MW01282206

Advance Praise

"If you and your team are in the business of building trusted relationships with people, then you recognize the challenge of understanding the psychology behind their often-irrational behavior. Kristian Aloma has been a student and practitioner of psychology and behavior within the context of branding and marketing for years and has identified a profound unlock through the power of story. Aloma is an accessible academic, effortlessly simplifying complex constructs so that we can move forward on actions that matter."

—DAVE HEALING, SENIOR DIRECTOR OF BRAND
STRATEGY & ACTIVATION AT ZILLOW GROUP

"Kristian Aloma knows his stuff. He is a uniquely talented analyst who has been studying the consumer mind for decades. Now that he has decided to share his expertise with the rest of us, we will all be smarter and better prepared to grow trust, activate customers, and shape behavior. This is an unmissable book for anyone looking to build a brand that matters."

—BRIAN REICH, AUTHOR, SPEECHWRITER,
AND COMMUNICATIONS STRATEGIST

Start with the Story

Start with the Story

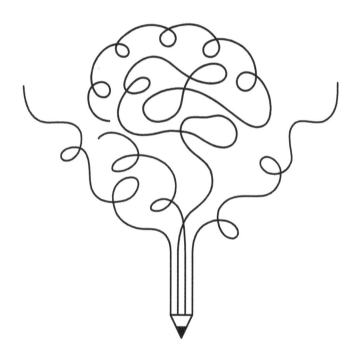

**BRAND-BUILDING IN
A NARRATIVE ECONOMY**

Kristian A Alomá, PhD

LIONCREST
PUBLISHING

START WITH THE STORY
Brand-Building in a Narrative Economy

FIRST EDITION

ISBN   978-1-5445-3736-8   *Hardcover*
        978-1-5445-3737-5   *Paperback*
        978-1-5445-3738-2   *Ebook*
        978-1-5445-4092-4   *Audiobook*

This book is dedicated to my partner, Courtney, and our two children, Athen and Avery. You are the beginning, middle, and end of my favorite stories.

Contents

Introduction

Marketing makes me angry.

Skin care ads tell customers the only way they'll be beautiful is if they use their products to improve their complexion. Insurance companies play up the risks of tragedy, leading customers to pursue purchases out of anxiety rather than security. Toy manufacturers tell children which toys are for girls and which are for boys, causing subtle shame when a child wants to play with a toy designed for another gender. It saddens me to see campaigns built on emotional exploitation.

As a brand strategist with a PhD in psychology, I've watched our industry largely use psychology to manipulate behavior, rather than inspire action. The above examples reveal marketing at its worst. But you don't have to look far to recognize how our industry has leveraged a cold and Pavlovian approach to marketing. We've largely treated consumers like hungry animals, trying to associate our products and services with the stimulus that gets them to salivate. We look for certain words and images that will trigger the desired response, no matter the impact on the customer.

If a Pavlovian relationship with your customers feels wrong, you're likely to agree with what I say next.

- **Marketing can feel disingenuous.** It can seem like the bottom line is the only metric that matters, and I wonder if it has to be that way.
- **Marketing can be manipulative.** I worry that some of the tactics used in marketing are unfair to the customer.
- **Marketers don't always think about the customer's best interests.** Sometimes I wonder whether we're doing right by the customer and am concerned that I'm complacent in tactics that don't fully represent me or my organization.

So many marketers tell me they feel deflated. They worry that making a sale is more important than making a positive impact in someone's life. Or growing the business and doing what's best for the customer are mutually exclusive. We often treat the customer as an afterthought or a data point to track, rather than the focus of our efforts as marketers.

But while the ethical concerns I have about marketing are what I feel most passionate about, that's not the only problem today's marketers face.

- **Traditional marketing is inconsistent.** Something that works one week might not the next.
- **Traditional marketing is unpredictable.** This industry

is temperamental, so even when I get something right, it doesn't mean it will continue to work in the future.

- **Traditional marketing feels like gambling.** Sometimes I feel like I'm throwing darts at a dartboard, but the value of the bullseye is constantly in flux.

If you agreed with those statements to any degree, you're not alone. I talk with marketers from all over the world who feel the exact same way. Marketers want more predictability. They want more certainty or clarity so that they can confidently build a new initiative. Yet no matter how many frameworks they use to define their marketing strategy, there's one factor that always throws a wrench in even the best-laid plans:

Human beings.

Their behavior can be unpredictable. Their emotions can be complex and difficult to understand. And their choices can appear illogical or irrational. The result is a marketing strategy that works great one week, but for no obvious reason flops the next. Marketing to these customers with traditional frameworks is like loading a ship with cargo but not equipping it with any sails. It will inevitably drift and might find land, but it will be no thanks to the captain.

Inconsistent and imprecise results are a major problem, considering that the goal of marketing is to attract the right people, motivate them to take a specific action, and inspire loyalty... over and over again. We need a clearer and more complete understanding of how people think to do our jobs effectively.

The good news is it is possible to meet and exceed your goals without sacrificing your conscience. You can build campaigns that are predictable and effective. You can do right by the customer *and* build a profitable company. And there is no role better suited to accomplishing both than you, the marketer.

BUILDING A BETTER BRAND

What is a "better brand," anyway?

It is both effective and mutually beneficial. It's built on the understanding that the customer is a person, not just a consumer. And when we prioritize the relationship between a company and its loyal fans in our marketing plans, we can do the impossible: we can harmoniously exceed the bottom line *and* positively impact the customer.

Historically, psychology hasn't been an integral part of the marketing framework. We need a new model that relates to the customer in a meaningful way—that uses principles of psychology to weave a company into customers' lives.

This methodology isn't a cheap tactic or manipulative trick. It isn't a clever way to push poor products onto unsuspecting consumers. And it's not a quick fix. If you're a marketer who is looking to move product as quickly as possible, this isn't the right book for you.

This book is for marketers who recognize that building brands is a social science. For those who understand that the decisions we make as marketers and brand-builders impact the way people feel about themselves, whether it's positive or negative. This book is for those who know that our identities are tied to the objects we own, the services we hire, and the companies that offer them.

Today my company Threadline uses the framework you'll learn about in this book for clients from all kinds of industries, all over the world. From the research we conduct with consumers to the conversations we have with everyone from salespeople to the CEO, we hear about how they are motivated by something bigger and more meaningful than the bottom line. Most marketers and customer-facing professionals just like helping people. Improving their lives. Making them smile.

There is no one better positioned to make a positive change in marketing than you. You are the bridge between business objectives and human impact, products and services and their role in people's lives, financial transactions and personal relationships. You are the key to better businesses built on better brands.

Together, we can redefine what it means to be a marketer, build a brand, and grow a business. We can root our practices in the social sciences and approach brand-building with as much rigor, structure, and care as a psychologist does their patients. Marketing impacts everyone and marketers wield incredible power. That's why I love this work and why I'm also so humbled by it. Once you understand the impact of your company in your customers' lives, you realize the responsibility of marketing is both to the success of the organization and the well-being of its customers.

Ultimately, this book is for those who recognize that a brand can do so much more than sell a product. It is for those who want to make a positive impact on people, their communities, and the world.

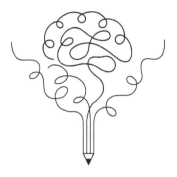

Chapter One

Welcome to the Narrative Economy

I began my PhD after years of working for an emotional branding agency. It was an extension of more than a decade of advising clients on how consumers felt about their products or services. So when I began developing my dissertation, I knew I wanted to formally unpack the minds of consumers. Repeatedly, my literature reviews led to one place: identity. Consumers—people—do nearly everything they do either because of their identity or to shape their identity.[1] As I unpacked the frameworks and insights around identity, I was introduced to a field of psychology that would eventually transform how I view the world.

Narrative psychology is a subset of psychology that looks at

---

1   Donald E. Polkinghorne, "Narrative and Self-Concept," *Journal of Narrative and Life History* 1, no. 2–3 (January 1991): 135–153, https://doi.org/10.1075/jnlh.1.2-3.04nar.

the way people make sense of themselves and their place in the world through the structure of story. We process our past, engage with the present, and predict the future using stories.[2] Our memories are episodic.[3] Our cultures are story-based.[4] Our immersion in stories is so complete that we may not even realize we're in a story until we're yanked out of it.

Narrative psychology tells us that we are constantly managing, updating, and tweaking the story that defines who we are. We tell stories that make sense of the things we do. And we do things that make sense of the stories we've told ourselves.[5] A story that says you're environmentally conscious explains why you use reusable cloth bags at the grocery store. And you continue to use them because that behavior fits within the narrative that you are environmentally conscious. These are stories about major life milestones, personal relationships, and ultimately identity. These aren't necessarily stories that people tell anyone else or that they verbally articulate, but rather stories unfolding in the mind. We aren't just storytellers—we're story-*thinkers*.

I went to Target to buy a new vacuum a while back. I saw Dyson, Black & Decker, and Shark on the shelves. At face value, I looked at the physical shape of the products and noticed details on

---

2   Polkinghorne, "Narrative and Self-Concept."

3   Endel Tulving, "Episodic Memory: From Mind to Brain," *Annual Review of Psychology* 53 (2002): 1–25, https://doi.org/10.1146/annurev.psych.53.100901.135114.

4   Joseph Campbell, *The Hero with a Thousand Faces*, 2nd ed. (Bollingen Series/Princeton: Princeton University Press, 1968): 1.

5   Donald E. Polkinghorne, "Narrative Psychology and Historical Consciousness Relationships and Perspectives," in *Narrative, Identity, and Historical Consciousness*, ed. Jürgen Straub (New York: Berghahn Books, 2005): 3–22, https://doi.org/10.1515/9781782388609-003.

colors and price. But I also subconsciously created the various stories I could tell about myself by owning each.

The classic vacuum with the fabric bag says that I like retro things or that the 1950s stereotypical mom thing is my vibe. On the other hand, the fancy Dyson model with the cyclone suction power says I care about design or technology. The Shark model might say I care about design and aesthetic, but in a more affordable package. Each tells a different story about who I am.

If you checked out my YouTube history, you'd learn that I love to travel. I follow two channels of travel vloggers. Both are van lifers, the term for people who buy vans that are retrofitted to function as homes in very, very tiny mobile packages.

One vlogger bought a lavish, brand-new Mercedes-Benz Sprinter van. The other bought a vintage 1976 Coachmen RV. Each vehicle performed a similar function but let the purchasers tell a very different story about themselves.

If we look at narrative psychology and consumerism simultaneously, we can understand how the products we buy help us express and shape that identity. If our consumer choices are driven in an effort to help us manage and express identity, and that identity is expressed through narrative, then the world operates on a narrative economy.[6] It is no longer about the exchange of goods and resources, it's about the exchange of stories for resources. We don't just buy goods and services, but rather buy the ability to tell a story. We purchase a way to shape our identity.

---

6   Jennifer Edson Escalas, "Narrative Processing: Building Consumer Connections to Brands," *Journal of Consumer Psychology* 14, no. 1–2 (2004): 168–180, https://doi.org/10.1207/s15327663jcp1401&2_19.

YOU ARE WHAT YOU OWN

From a rational perspective, the Porsche Cayenne shouldn't exist.

Owning a Porsche is about driving something fast, powerful, luxurious, and a little dangerous. It markets to young, single, successful professionals who take risks and collect big rewards. A Porsche helps them express and celebrate success. A person buys a Porsche because they look cool, drive fast, and are well out of most people's price range.

So, what happens when that young, single, risk-taker gets older, has a family, and needs to slow down? Most of the time, they reluctantly turn in their Porsche for what is essentially the antithesis of a Porsche—an affordable minivan with three times the airbags and a built-in baby cam that lets you see that adorable baby strapped securely into the back seat. While their baby crawls around with another during a playdate, they vent to the other parents about the car they used to have and the life they used to live.

Psychologists would call them "conflicted." They were faced with a tension between two identities: the first being the wealthy professional that lives life to the fullest and the other of a responsible parent. These two identities couldn't coexist in a single vehicle, so customers chose to buy a different vehicle (rather than getting rid of their kids) and deal with the cognitive dissonance by repeatedly reminding their neighbors how cool they used to be.

Considering this tension, the Porsche Cayenne couldn't help but appeal to this crowd. It has the look, name, and expense of a Porsche, but in a safer and more responsible package. Four doors with plenty of room for the car seat *and* the groceries.

Now that professional can tell the world and themselves that they are successful enough to drive a Porsche, *and* that they are a responsible parent.

The Cayenne is just one example of how products impact our identities. Years ago, I conducted in-home interviews about health-conscious dietary choices. My research partners and I spoke to people who were hardcore into an organic lifestyle. They only drank and stored water in glass bottles. Their fridges were full of organic fruits and vegetables. Everything in their pantry was from Trader Joe's or Whole Foods.

At least, *almost* everything.

I asked a participant to open the cabinet to record which products they had on their shelves. I was surprised when between a refillable jar of wild rice and whole wheat linguine was a box of Kraft Mac & Cheese.

"Tell me about how you've stocked your shelves," I prompted, genuinely intrigued. I was truly fascinated as to how that box got there. Was it left by a friend? Was it a decade old and a remnant from college days? Or was this person about to tout the health benefits of eating processed foods?

On the contrary, this person was well aware that the cheese inside the little foil packets wasn't naturally that yellow. They knew the pasta wasn't organic. They weren't duped. They never tried to defend the ingredient list.

Instead, they smiled and said, "We know it's weird, but it's our boxed comfort."

As we talked, I discovered that they didn't really see the macaroni product as food at all. It wasn't nutrition or fuel for their bodies, it was a metaphorical warm blanket fresh out of the dryer or a burning candle on a rainy day. It was comfort, not nutrition. It was a box of stress relief that can only come from a warm bowl of fake yellow pasta. They knew that sometimes the organic, health-conscious food that fits their everyday lifestyle just doesn't work when they feel like things are falling apart at work.

Helping parents feel cool or young adults feel comforted are just some of the ways companies help us manage our identity. In research with participants, I've learned about products used to create thousands of different narratives. And after reflecting on those stories and the findings from dozens of peer-reviewed papers, I started to see a clear pattern about how consumers use products and services. Most of them fit into one of four roles.

THE FOUR ROLES OF BRANDS IN CONSUMER IDENTITY

In my academic work and review of the literature, I've concluded there are four roles of consumer goods and services in consumer identity. They include expression/differentiation, resolution, exploration/expansion, and affirmation.[7] Understanding how and when to use each can unlock the incredible link between businesses and identity. Below is a description and an example of each.

---

7   Bernd Schmitt, "The Consumer Psychology of Brands," *Journal of Consumer Psychology* 22, no. 1 (January 2012): 7–17, https://doi.org/10.1016/j.jcps.2011.09.005.

1. EXPRESSION/DIFFERENTIATION

These products or services help us tell the world who we are. What we stand for. What we love. They help us define who we are and who we are not.

Nutella: I don't just like chocolate or peanut butter. I like what Europeans like. I like a sophisticated, decadent, indulgent spread for my toast. I am cultured.

2. RESOLUTION

These products or services help consumers cross multiple identities such as mother and professional, caregiver and partner, father and husband. Where identities sometimes conflict, these companies help resolve that tension.

Willow Breast Pumps: I am a mom that cares about breastfeeding, but I hate being tied to a wall like a charging device. I'm also a woman and homeowner, and have errands to run other than emptying my breasts. I can be independent and supportive of my family and ambitions.

3. EXPLORATION/EXPANSION

These products or services help us expand our sense of self either through what they provide or being outside of our comfort zone. Sometimes these products are trials that become permanent.

Duolingo: I am a lover of languages and someone who appreciates other cultures. I want to expand my identity by becoming someone who is multilingual.

4. AFFIRMATION

Some products or services remind us who we are. They help us prove to ourselves we are who we want to be. Though affirmation can look and feel similar to expression, its target is different. Expression is for others. Affirmation is for ourselves.

SpotHero: I am a savvy city dweller that won't be duped into paying ridiculous prices for parking.

But building a product or service and impacting identity don't just happen. People are protective of their identity. They don't let just anyone or anything become part of it—just as few people let a guy on the street with a tattoo gun ink their mother's name on their chest. To become part of someone's identity, you have to be more than just a thing they buy. You have to build a relationship.

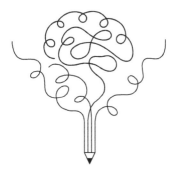

Chapter Two

Building Relationships

Once you get a federal tax ID, open a bank account, and source a product or service to sell, you have a business.

But it doesn't mean you have a *brand*.

So what is a brand, anyway?

If you ask a marketer, they might say a brand is the representation of a business. If you ask an academic, they might say it's a theme. If you ask your uncle, he might say it's a logo. It seems that no one can agree on what a brand actually is.[8] But despite the fact that few people can define it, almost everyone can recognize when one exists. Apple users will pay hundreds of dollars more than they would for similar products offered

---

8   Leslie de Chernatony and Francesca Dall'Olmo Riley, "Defining a 'Brand': Beyond the Literature with Experts' Interpretations," *Journal of Marketing Management* 14, no. 5 (1998): 417–443, https://doi.org/10.1362/026725798784867798.

by competitors, stand in line for hours to buy the latest gadget, and defend the company tirelessly against Android fans.

Harley-Davidson riders drive their bikes for days to celebrate at rallies all over the world, obsess over the newest models, and even get tattoos of the logo.

Patagonia customers often pay double the price of similar items and proudly display the logo on their outdoor gear. When the company missteps, fans vehemently defend its position as one of the most iconic and ethical gear companies of all time.

Why do people fall in love with businesses like Apple, Harley-Davidson, and Patagonia? Why do they loyally defend them on social media, in reviews, and over dinner, the way they might a good friend? Why will people pay more for a product with the exact same features as its competitors? Why do they graciously continue to support a company, even after a mistake?

The simple answer is a good brand. A good brand makes marketing easier, more effective, more reliable, and more productive.

But the definition that makes the most sense when studying consumers at a psychological level describes a brand as the *relationship* between a business and its customers. That means you do not have a brand until you build a relationship with your customer *beyond* the product or service you sell.

What is your relationship with Dawn dish soap like?

For a lot of people, they bought Dawn when they moved out of their parents' house because it's the same product they grew up with. And maybe they kept buying it because it works well and is inexpensive. But after the oil spill in the Gulf, people had a new reason to keep buying the product. Their relationship with Dawn shifted from functional and nostalgic to functional and value signaling. And Dawn is likely to emphasize that element of the relationship even when there isn't an oil-covered seagull to rescue. Because when it comes to its relationship with consumers, its role is to help clean the dishes *and* help consumers feel good about using the product. Knowing the soap on their kitchen counter was also used to rescue animals is a part of the relationship between Dawn and its customers.

I love McDonald's, and it's not a joke. Even with some of the finest restaurants around the corner, if you were to ask me which is my absolute favorite, I will almost always tell you McDonald's. And it's not because I think the Big Mac should be Michelin rated or that the French fries are the best ever made. It's because the restaurant created a space where my family could treat themselves.

When I was a child my grandparents would take me and my brothers to McDonald's every Saturday. On the way there they'd teach us Spanish vocabulary. When we arrived ten minutes later, we could order a Happy Meal or a burger. (I remember the rite of passage when my grandparents thought I was old enough to finally handle a Big Mac.) After we finished eating, we would play on the playground. At the end, we had a tradition of touching every structure in the PlayPlace and then jumping to high-five the life-size Ronald McDonald waving to the street. On the way home, we'd practice more Spanish and spend the evening watching *Golden Girls* and *Empty Nest* until it was time to go home. For me, McDonald's isn't just a restaurant. It's a part of the memories and stories I tell about my late grandparents. I have a relationship with McDonald's that is so deep that to this day, I get as excited as my kids when I tell them we're going to McDonald's.

You might not be a McDonald's or a Dawn. I chose those examples because they are familiar to a wide audience, but that doesn't mean that a niche company can't form a dynamic relationship with its customers. There's a small cookie shop in Amsterdam that isn't much bigger than a king-size bed. There's room for perhaps eight people to stand in line in the store. They only make one cookie, a rich dark chocolate dough with a decadent piece of white chocolate baked into the middle.

If you're ever walking around the canals of Amsterdam and find a line that runs down a block and over one of the canals, you've likely discovered Van Stapele Koekmakerij and the best damn cookie you'll ever find outside my own family's oven.

But Van Stapele Koekmakerij has created more than the perfect cookie, it's created an experience that feels like Vera van Stapele is handing you the cookies and giving you a little hug every time. Their shop is adorable, their cookies are delicious, the tin box they package them in is the sort of keepsake you want to leave out for others to see. Even the directions they include tell you to warm the cookies by placing them on a warm radiator for a few minutes. From the moment you become a customer, you know this is a relationship you want to keep. And now my home in Chicago has at least two empty tins to refill on my next trip to Amsterdam. For my daughter, it's perhaps her symbol—and most cherished memory—of our trip to Amsterdam.

Building a relationship with customers is the path to long-term success as a business. That's when customers can start to form meaningful relationships that are more than just one thing. A relationship can evolve as the customer does. Lego meant one thing to you as a kid but can mean something else to you as an adult. Kraft Mac & Cheese can mean something to you in childhood, another during early adulthood, and yet another if or when you have children of your own. The relationships we form with companies can be like the ones we form with people: they can grow, change, and adapt.

Now that you've considered the powerful relationship a business can build with a customer, it's time to evaluate the one your company has with your customers.

EIGHT ELEMENTS OF A RELATIONSHIP

After studying interpersonal relationships and consumers, I've discovered that many of the principles that help us understand the relationships we have with other people are relevant to the relationships we have with the products or services we consume. I've identified seven elements of a relationship and they are categorized in three buckets: behavioral, social, and alignment. Some you'll likely recognize in a business context, but I expect you'll find new insight through the lens of psychology. You'll also see many traits on this list that you've likely never associated with a product because they are decidedly *human*-to-*human* interactions. And while they may surprise you, they'll also offer a new perspective on how your business relates to your customers.

BEHAVIORAL ELEMENTS

The behavioral elements of a relationship are about how the consumer engages with the product or service. It is the first level of the relationship because it is the easiest to accomplish but also limited in terms of how deep a relationship can be built from behavior alone. However, without the behavioral elements it will be difficult to build a relationship at all. You have to show up and you have to perform. While consumer relationships can be emotional, they can't be if they're not first practical.

Frequency of Interaction

Frequency of interaction refers to how often your consumer uses or engages with your product or service.

Just as in personal relationships, we tend to build strong relationships with products or services we interact with often.[9] The frequency allows for exposure, and exposure breeds familiarity and comfort. Much like the delivery man who shows up every week with packages, you start to develop a basic relationship. It's cordial and friendly, though it still has some distance and boundary.

Consider the frequency you interact with the milk you add to your coffee every morning or the shampoo you use every day.

---

9   Kristian A. Alomá, "The Impact of Time and Frequency of Use on Self-Brand Overlap" (PhD diss., Fielding Graduate University, 2019), https://www.proquest.com/openview/ba42168f4f9fda0357ddf e087cde957b/1?pq-origsite=gscholar&cbl=18750&diss=y.

Variety of Interaction

The variety of interaction refers to the various ways the consumer interacts with your product or service.

When products or services show up in multiple areas of our lives, they can feel like a reliable presence or a consistent face. Beyond familiarity, this variety of interaction begins to open the door to new kinds of interactions, a broader set of experiences, and a more diverse relationship.

Think about all the various ways you use Amazon. You might purchase household items and clothing, but you might also stream media or even fill your prescriptions through its pharmacy.

Depth of Interaction

The depth of interaction speaks to how significant the interaction might be.

Like friends we don't see often, products or services that are part of meaningful or important parts of our lives don't have to show up frequently or in a variety of ways. But the role they play in specific, personally important or meaningful moments adds weight to the relationship.

A life insurance agent, family physician, international airline, or your favorite salon are examples of a meaningful interaction with a business. Though they might not serve a variety of roles or be a constant presence, you can still form a strong relationship with them because of the meaningful roles they fill.

Length of Relationship

Experiences take time. And time allows for an organization to demonstrate loyalty, capability, and reliability, which are the key elements of trust.

Many people tend to have a long relationship with laundry detergent, using what their parents used through college and into adulthood. The local mechanic shop that has worked on your car ever since you knew how to drive has a long relationship. The barber shop you tried once after you moved in has only a short relationship.

Time is relative, so whether someone perceives the relationship as long or short may be dependent on the usage patterns or the age of the industry overall. Long relationships can be those that have been around since childhood, like my relationship with McDonald's, or just a few years, like your relationship with your favorite pair of earbuds.

The frequency and variety of interaction, as well as the length of the relationship, are all behavioral elements of a relationship between a consumer and a company. But there is much more to a relationship than what we do. The next elements of a relationship fall under the category of social or communal.

SOCIAL/CONNECTION ELEMENTS

Social and communal elements of a relationship are about the connections between a company and a consumer and how they feel about those connections. These move the relationship deeper and often take some time or resources to develop.

Belonging

Some products or services can create a sense of community among their consumers. Communities, or social groups, help consumers determine who they are and where they belong.

Consider the community around Peloton exercise bikes. There are Peloton Facebook groups and workout clubs. There are Peloton workouts on YouTube and Instagram. Peloton has created an entire social group around their stationary bikes.

Trust

Trust demonstrates a shared sense of risk and reward between two parties. Between organizations and consumers, it's evidence that the organization is willing to do right by the customer and the customer is willing to be loyal to the organization. Trust can take time to build and often requires doing extra and holding your business accountable.

Once trust is built, it's difficult to break. And it often opens the doors to deeper relationships and more vulnerable experiences.

It takes belonging and trust to form a communal or social connection between a company and a customer. But a relationship doesn't stop there. The final layer of relationships is alignment.

ALIGNMENT ELEMENTS

Alignment is when relationships begin to shift toward shared ideas, values, and experiences. The more consumers feel they share with an organization, the more likely they are to feel close to that organization. This level can have the most impact on a relationship.

Similarity in Personality

Organizations have personalities just like people. Sometimes they're considered sweet, funny, or intelligent. The more the consumer has in common—or wants to have in common—the more willing they may be to invest in the relationship.

Personalities demonstrate a shared way of approaching the world. And similar personalities can make us feel comfortable because we know what to expect. Further, relationships allow people to share or acquire the traits of others.[10] Companies that have aspirational personalities, such as confidence, can share those traits with their consumers until the consumer feels them entirely on their own.

Banana Republic exudes a young yet sophisticated confidence and therefore allows its customers to adopt similar qualities. Smart electric vehicles are forward-thinking and green, which allows its customers to assume those same attributes.

Similarity in Values

An organization's values help communicate what it cares about, what it stands for, and what it's willing to sacrifice to uphold.

---

10   Rebecca K. Trump and Merrie Brucks, "Overlap between Mental Representations of Self and Brand," *Self and Identity* 11, no. 4 (2012): 454–471, https://doi.org/10.1080/15298868.2011.595083.

Consumers often look for organizations that share their values so that they can feel consistent in their personal beliefs.[11]

When we make choices, we implicitly endorse the business we consume. Therefore consumers can be very sensitive to the values expressed by the organization. The more aligned or aspirational it is, the more likely the consumer is to invest. Consider what it meant when Nike endorsed Colin Kaepernick. Some consumers felt they shared values of justice with Nike. Others burned their shoes.

Let's take inventory of what you've uncovered so far. First, identity is connected to what we consume, meaning the things we buy and the services we hire. Second, we make sense of that identity through story. The narrative economy that we live in is built on the stories the things we buy enable us to tell about ourselves. And finally, to impact that story, you must first build a relationship with your consumer. The next chapter is a diagnostic that will uncover the strength of that relationship and ultimately, the health of your brand.

11   Giusy Buonfantino, "New Research Shows Consumers More Interested in Brands' Values than Ever," Google Cloud Blog, April 27, 2022, https://cloud.google.com/blog/topics/consumer-packaged-goods/data-shows-shoppers-prioritizing-sustainability-and-values.

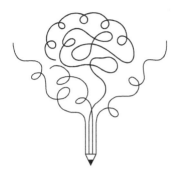

Chapter Three

Health-Check Your Relationship

I didn't always drink Oatly. Like a lot of people, I was raised on cow's milk. My transition began when I first wondered whether drinking cow's milk regularly aligns with my desire to be more environmentally conscious. I then researched the environmental impact of dairy cows. From there, I looked for alternatives like coconut, soy, and almond. But coconut milk was high in trans fat, soy milk tasted weird with cereal, and almond milk wasn't that environmentally friendly either.

Oat milk seemed to be the most environmentally conscientious based on how little water is used to produce it. It was also the non-dairy milk that didn't overwhelm you with some other flavor. But that's what drove me to oat milk. In the end, I chose Oatly because the packaging, design, and messaging all felt like it didn't take itself too seriously. It aligned with how I realistically thought my milk choice would affect global warming. I'm not fooling myself into believing oat milk can solve the climate crisis. I'm just making an individual choice that I think is important. And the Oatly personality sort of recognized that through their comic-inspired graphics and how they labeled the nutrition info "the boring (but very important) side." It helped that my kids thought it was funny, too.

Whether it happened intentionally or by mistake, your customers have a relationship with your business. The following quiz will help give you a reading on the health of that relationship so that you can see where your brand excels and where it needs more attention. Consider this a clinical assessment by a couples counselor—but for brands.

Ready to find out what your relationship with your consumers looks like? Answer the following questions as honestly as you can from the perspective of your consumer. If your answer falls somewhere between answers, I recommend being conservative and rounding down. Be ready to calculate your answer at the bottom of the quiz.

How frequently do your customers use or engage with your product or service?

1. Less than once a year
2. Once a year
3. Once a quarter
4. Once a month
5. Once a week
6. Once a day
7. Multiple times a day

In how many ways does your customer use or engage with your product or service?

1. One way and one way only
2. A couple of ways
3. We show up in a few places
4. We're used in several ways
5. We're there in most parts of their life
6. They rely on us quite a bit
7. They almost can't survive without us

How would your customer describe the significance of using your product in their life?

1. Very unimportant or meaningless
2. Somewhat unimportant or meaningless
3. Unimportant or meaningless
4. Neither unimportant/important nor meaningless/meaningful
5. Important or meaningful
6. Somewhat important or meaningful
7. Very important or meaningful

Compared to the industry or category of your product or service, how long has your customer been using or engaging with your business? (This question is intentionally relative. For some industries three years may be a lifetime, for others it may take twenty years.)

1. The shortest time compared to our industry
2. A very short time compared to our industry
3. A short time compared to our industry
4. An average amount of time compared to our industry

5. A long time compared to our industry
6. A very long time compared to our industry
7. The longest time compared to our industry

How connected do your customers feel to you or a community of other customers?

1. Our customers don't feel connected in any way with other customers
2. Our customers recognize other customers may have something in common but don't want to connect with them
3. Our customers will connect to other customers, but they don't seek it out
4. Our customers feel a close kinship with other customers
5. Our customers will describe themselves as part of our community
6. Our customers voluntarily contribute to or engage with our community
7. Our customers have created a fan club centered around our business

How much do your customers believe you care about their best interests beyond the financial value they provide?

1. Our customers don't think we care at all
2. Our customers aren't sure what to expect from us
3. Our customers only expect we'll deliver what they paid for but nothing more
4. Our customers expect us to deliver on what we promised but assume it will be difficult to get any more than that
5. If our customers ask, they know we will try to solve any issues they've shared with us

6. If we're aware of a problem, our customers know we will do whatever it takes to make it right

7. Our customers know we will go above and beyond even before they ask

How similarly do your business and your customers think and act (intellectual, humorous, serious)?

1. Our customers do not think and act like we do at all
2. There are almost no similarities between how we and our customers think and act
3. There are very few similarities between how we and our customers think and act
4. There are similarities between how we and our customers think and act but nothing notable
5. There are some similarities between how we and our customers think and act
6. There are a lot of similarities between how we and our customers think and act
7. Our customers think and act exactly like we do

How much do your customers think your values align with their own?

1. Our values do not align at all
2. Our values are not very aligned
3. Our values are slightly less aligned than average
4. Our values are more or less aligned
5. Our values are slightly more aligned than average
6. Our values are very aligned
7. Our values are perfectly aligned

Tally each answer, assigning it a score that corresponds with its number in the list. The higher the score, the more likely you are to have a deep, meaningful relationship with your customer. The deeper your relationship, the more likely you are to have a brand. The lower the score, the opposite is true. You may have a useful product or service, but not much beyond that.

Here's a quick breakdown that should provide you with some directional insight into the kind of relationship you have:

SCORE OF 8: FAMILIAR STRANGER

There is essentially no relationship between you and your customer. This is about as low as you can go and still sell a product or service. They know you exist and have made at least one choice to purchase you, but there is no expectation the relationship will or should go any deeper. In some cases, they may not want it to go any deeper. Think about that random product you purchased off that Instagram ad.

SCORE OF 9-16: ACQUAINTANCE

Your customers have developed a relationship with you, but it isn't very strong. You may either perform well in a couple of areas or just okay in all of them. Still, it's better than nothing. If they recognized you in a crowd, they may awkwardly wave. If you're not a car person, think about the battery you bought when your last one died.

SCORE OF 17-24: COLLEAGUE

You're building a relationship now, but it's still pretty distant.

They expect more from you and you show up more often in their lives, however, there are definitely boundaries. Think about the company you may have hired to spray for bugs at your home. You pay for their service but you're never home when they show up.

SCORE OF 25-32: CLOSE CONNECTION

This is a pretty solid relationship for most companies. You're considered trustworthy but you're not getting a holiday card mailed to you or invited to the group chat. There's a lot of potential at this level. Think about that shop where you get your bicycle tuned up—friendly folks who you will bring your bike to again.

SCORE OF 33-40: FRIEND

You've made it. You and your customer have quite a bit in common and you're close enough to be considered a part of the group. Now you're in the chat. Word of mouth is likely to be pretty good. And there's a decent bit of resilience to the relationship. You're definitely invited to the BBQ. Think of the business where you get your hair cut every 6–8 weeks.

SCORE OF 41-48: INNER CIRCLE

Things are pretty serious at this point and there's likely to be a great deal of trust built into the relationship. You're the first to hear about life changing events and they're willing to share more of their life with you. You're not only at the BBQ, but your families might also vacation together. If you've had dry skin your whole life, think of the lotion you swear by.

SCORE OF 49-56: PLATONIC SOULMATE

You two are so aligned you're almost reading each other's minds. You care about the same things—and one another—more than most other things or people in your life. They know your secrets, your fears, and your most honest ambitions. If you're here, you're pretty set already. (Why did you pick up this book?) Think about the company logo you have tattooed on your chest.

Of course, not every business's logo is tattooed on its customer's bicep. So the quiz will likely have highlighted strengths and weaknesses that could be holding your company back from making those truly meaningful relationships that you dream about as a marketer. And in some cases, you don't need to become a platonic soulmate to succeed. Great businesses exist in almost all levels above Familiar Stranger. But if you want to build real loyalty, you'll want to go deeper.

Understanding the aspects of a great relationship is one thing. But feeling in control of them is another. And even if you have a great relationship, you should ask about the role you play in that relationship. Are you the friend they know can always cheer them up? Are you the person in the inner circle that gives them the pep talk before the big meeting? Or are you the platonic soulmate that knows when they need a hug instead of advice? It can feel like something that should arise organically, or at the very least, something that the company has very little influence over. But the best company-customer relationships are carefully and intentionally designed.

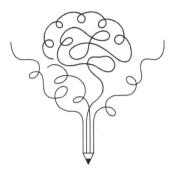

Chapter Four

The Core Principles of Narrative Design

If you wanted to bake a cake before the 1930s, you'd go to the store to buy flour, sugar, butter, and any other ingredients. Then you'd sift the flour, measure the sugar, take care not to overmix, pop it in the oven, and hope it didn't collapse as soon as you put it on the counter to cool. Cake wasn't terribly difficult to make, but it did take time and effort.

The first iteration of boxed cake mix required the baker to simply add oil and water. No need to overthink shopping, measuring, or baking time. It was all on the box. And you know what? It usually turned out better than cake from scratch.

Considering the ease to bake and the quality of the product, you would think cake mix would have been an instant hit, right? Just a fraction of the time with even better results.

What's not to love? The only problem was that no one bought it. And the reason may surprise you.

In the thirties, cakes were baked predominantly by women with families. And the act of baking was seen as an act of love—particularly *because* baking is time consuming. Based on the problematic reasoning of that era, if you take the expertise and time out of the equation, it isn't really baking. And if she isn't really baking, does she even love her family? Consumers didn't buy the product because it wasn't tasty, but because it didn't align with the narrative they wanted to tell.

As sexist and bizarre as that last paragraph is, it doesn't change the fact that society simply did not consider the boxed mix cooking. So how could the business regain control of the narrative?

They discovered that if they took the powdered egg out of the mix so that the consumer would have to go through the process of cracking and stirring a fresh one in, it suddenly felt more like baking. The egg changed everything. Suddenly housewives could tell themselves that they were still baking—and loving—their family.[12]

Common sense suggests that the most convenient item would yield the highest return. And if we were rational decision makers, this would be true. But we're humans. And we didn't want the easiest possible cake, we wanted the easiest possible cake *that still felt like baking.*

---

12   Michael Y. Park, "A History of the Cake Mix, the Invention That Redefined 'Baking'," *Bon Appétit*, September 26, 2013, https://www.bonappetit.com/entertaining-style/pop-culture/article/cake-mix-history.

Narrative design allows us to create the right conditions for our customers *to tell the stories they want to tell about themselves.* But it's not storytelling in the traditional sense. To understand the nuance of narrative design, we first have to separate narrative from story.

NARRATIVE VS. STORY

In everyday life we use the terms narrative and story interchangeably: a story is a narrative and a narrative is a story. However, in the context of narrative design, I want you to think of them as different: a story is the expression of a narrative. Narrative is the mannequin; the story is the dress.

The narrative is the underlying skeleton, the big idea, or the core way you want someone to make sense of your product or service. It's something that you directly control. One of my favorite examples of a narrative is from cinema: love always wins. So many great movies use various stories to dress up this narrative, from *Shrek* to *Titanic* to *The Notebook.* Each of these movies showcases a very different story written for widely different audiences, but they all are built on a singular narrative.

I've always loved cartoons. But now that I watch them with my children, I notice the two different stories being told simultaneously for two different audiences. The first story is designed for children, the second for adults. They are engaged and so am I, but for different reasons. We're all laughing at jokes, but rarely at the same ones. And if we do share a laugh over the same joke, it's unlikely to be for the same reason. In this way, children's movies are a great example of how something can be relevant for different audiences by telling different stories built on one narrative.

This is important because many companies focus on the story and ignore the narrative. They think, *what do we need to say to make them laugh* or *what do they find interesting?* By focusing first on the underlying narrative, companies can then determine which stories to tell and which stories they might inspire for their customers.

A great brand arises when you design for the narrative and then give your customers the space and freedom to tell their own individual stories. Build the mannequin and each customer can clothe it with their own style.

In effort to highlight the importance of understanding a problem, Einstein is often quoted as having said, "If I had only one hour to save the world, I would spend fifty-five minutes defining the problem, and only five minutes finding the solution." You want a similar balance when it comes to narrative and story. Spend most of your time carefully designing for the narrative. Then, listen to your customers' stories to ensure you've framed it in the right way.

Narrative
VS
Story

THE NARRATIVE DESIGN PROCESS

The next three points are a broad introduction to the process of narrative design. In the following chapters, we will further break these down so that you can plug and play your product or service into this framework. The narrative design process has three basic elements:

1. Understand the audience's story and the narrative beneath it (research)
2. Identify opportunities to shape/improve the narrative (strategy)
3. Propose a role for your organization in their narrative and help them tell their story (action/innovation)

Ultimately, understanding narrative design begins with understanding the audience through a process called psychobiographical research. Essentially, if you're going to find a role in someone else's story, you have to understand their story first. This is where research and insights at a level beyond demographic data is so important. You need to know what customers think about themselves, the role the category of your product or service plays in their lives, and what their relationship is to you.

When I became a dad, I realized that most companies are pretty bad at connecting with us. Every advertisement has the same old trope. Dad fumbling with diapers. Dad starting a fire in the kitchen. Dad being exhausted by parenthood. These commercials weren't truly thinking about me and their potential relationship with me. Their stories didn't resemble fatherhood or my experience with my children. Instead, they were trying to create a campaign that they thought people would find funny (they weren't). It's easy to spot businesses that are just trying to insert themselves into someone's story without a genuine connection.

The fundamental value of narrative design is realized in how an organization chooses to play a genuine role in their customer's story.

The question is, what kind of role do you want?

One of my clients is a company called LifeWeb 360. LifeWeb is a platform that generates digital memorials, allowing families to celebrate life and grieve together digitally. Their services were especially appreciated during the 2020 COVID-19 pandemic, when people were cut off from the usual grieving process of planning and attending a funeral with their loved ones.

Their online memorials provide people the opportunity to create a space that makes that story gathering more permanent and invites more people to participate in the celebration of that person's life. Even outside of the pandemic, LifeWeb 360 helps people who may not be able to attend share stories, videos, and photos.

When we asked people who used the platform what role LifeWeb 360 played in their lives, most said something like, "They helped turn what could have been an even more difficult moment—especially during a pandemic—into a broader celebration of life."

When you map out the audience's story, identify an opportunity to shape or improve the story, and then propose the role for your organization within that story, you design for narrative.

LifeWeb understood their audience. They decided the role and impact they wanted to have in that story. Then they delivered their narrative in the design of the interface, the wording of the messaging, and the product itself.

That's narrative design.

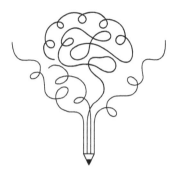

Chapter Five

The Mind of Your Customer

Traditional market research often feels like an interrogation. It's a battery of questions that researchers throw at you in surveys or in one-on-one interviews that can feel like you're trying to be caught in a lie. Why did you do that? What do you like about it? What would you want this to do instead? Which one do you like better? Would you buy this? Why? At best, it's uncomfortable. At worst, it leads marketers to make poor decisions based on faulty data.

The problem with traditional market research is that people don't always know why they do something. When someone is asked why they made a choice, the part of the brain that influences the decision isn't revealing its secrets. The mind is talented in many areas. Explaining itself to you is not one of them.

Historically, the entire field of economics considered human behavior in the marketplace as completely rational. Traditional economics looked at the world as buyers and ignored the fact that when consumers go home, they have emotions, love their families, and all those other pesky human traits. The economists just didn't care about that part because it's beyond the transaction.

The traditional economic model, however, ends up failing to predict actual behavior in the marketplace. Humans aren't cogs and wheels or robots responding to inputs. It wasn't until psychology butted its way into economics that we had a better understanding of how the economy works.

Behavioral economics started to identify that the people—the key players in an economic system—were human beings with minds and emotions and didn't necessarily do much of anything based on economic theories. We don't save enough in our 401(k)s. We panic-sell stock when the market is low and buy when it's at an all-time high. We gamble and purchase lottery tickets. We hoard piles of toilet paper during a pandemic.

The way we engage with the economy isn't rational—it's inherently emotional. Neuroscientist Antonio Damasio famously said that human beings are not thinking machines that feel, we are feeling machines that think.[13] Feeling machines require marketing to respond to their emotional needs as much as their rational needs.

In *Thinking, Fast and Slow,* author Daniel Kahneman describes

---

13   Antonio Damasio, *Self Comes to Mind: Constructing the Conscious Brain* (New York: Pantheon, 2010): 115.

humanity as operating on a two-system model: the fast and slow brain.[14] The fast brain is casually called the lizard brain, referring to the ancient part of the brain that reacts imperceptibly fast in response to stimuli. We'll call it System 1. It controls everything that happens behind the scenes, like respiratory function, digestion, and response to stimuli (to name a few).

System 1 also controls many of our actions. It's helpful to think of the fast brain as a three-year-old looking for candy. It's driven by impulse and emotion and changes its mind very quickly. *The fire was hot so I pulled my hand away. I tripped and caught myself. This person hurt my feelings, so I am angry. I'm stressed, so I made macaroni and cheese.* These thoughts are reflections of the fast brain.

But wait, you might think, *I am an intellectual adult engaging in the mysteries of the universe, marketing included! I'm in control and choosing to read this book right now, aren't I?*

The fact that you are reading these words is related to System 2, the slow brain. I often describe it to my clients as a middle-aged middle manager who wants to solve the Wordle every day. System 2 likes things to be neat, orderly, and clean. It loves logic and puzzles. It's responsible for high-order thinking, like metacognition (thinking about thinking), the ability to do math, or deriving pleasure from reading poetry. It's also responsible for making sense of the things that our fast brain does, like reaching for that box of macaroni even though our slow brain thinks it should have a salad.

---

14   Daniel Kahneman, *Thinking, Fast and Slow* (New York: Farrar, Straus and Giroux, 2011): 20.

Even though they operate side by side, Systems 1 and 2 don't necessarily understand each other. They just influence each other. One of the maxims of psychology that is universally true is that the best answer to almost any question about why we did something is "I don't know." The brain is not designed to know, but rather a system built for survival and energy preservation.

So when we ask someone a question in traditional market research, we're asking System 2 to explain both what it thinks and what System 1 thinks. And explaining what System 1 thinks is like explaining why you like an abstract painting or modern art. There really are no words that capture it. And no one really agrees whether it's even art.

Instead of trying to explain the meaning of art—or the nuance of our emotions—System 2 provides an answer it thinks the moderator will accept. In other words, we say whatever we think is the right answer. Of course, the right answer is not necessarily the true answer.

To bridge the gap between System 1 and System 2, we need to stop asking questions of System 2 that System 1 isn't privy to or understands. Instead, we need to conduct research in the language of the mind.

In the mid-2000s, researchers began to use functional magnetic resonance imaging (fMRI) technology, which can show how the brain reacts to stimuli in real time. This technology revealed that people connect to products at a deeper level than we realized.

One of the more famous experiments involved taste testing Coca-Cola vs. Pepsi. In the first level of testing, researchers hooked participants up to an fMRI machine while they drank either Coca-Cola or Pepsi. As one would expect, the brain responded differently based on whether they were Coke or Pepsi fans.[15]

The most interesting part of this study occurred during the last phase when researchers gave the participants two samples of soda, labeling one as Coca-Cola and mislabeling the other as a generic soda. In actuality, both cups contained Coke. Researchers wanted to find whether they responded differently to the mislabeled soda.

When the participants drank the Coke labeled as generic, a portion of the brain lit up associated with tasting and sensing. But when they drank from the cup labeled Coca-Cola, a wider area of the brain reacted. Participants didn't just connect to the taste and smell of the soda, but to memories of it in their lives. Participants were essentially tasting the soda and telling themselves stories at the same time. If we want to understand what the consumers really thought about the soda, we can't just ask them what it tasted like. We need to ask about those stories that lit up other areas of their brain.

The first step in narrative design is to get inside the mind of your customer using psychobiographical research. In this type of information gathering, researchers ask questions that help

15   Erin Green and Claire Murphy, "Altered Processing of Sweet Taste in the Brain of Diet Soda Drinkers," *Physiology & Behavior* 107, no. 4 (November 2012): 560–567, https://doi.org/10.1016/j.physbeh.2012.05.006.

reveal the stories at the heart of the relationship between customers and companies.

Over time, patterns emerge across stories; threads of ideas that repeat from person to person. Those threads become powerful insights for organizations that are trying to build stronger relationships.

THE SECRET TO PSYCHOBIOGRAPHICAL RESEARCH

When you approach market research from the narrative perspective, then you uncover what's really happening when your clients make decisions below the surface of their conscious thought. Stories and storytelling are so powerful in market research because they help us either disarm those psychological barriers or sidestep them cognitively.

When I ask someone, "Why did you purchase that soda" or "Why did you visit that store," they will answer that question as best as they know how to.

Likely the response will sound very rational, like, "It's in the mall near my house" or "I typically like their styles or their fashions" or "I was thirsty, and this soda was available and cold, so I decided to buy it." Those answers could hold some truth, but there is a world of insight left to uncover.

If I take a moment to reframe the question and ask someone to tell me about their experience purchasing a new shirt or tell me about the story of when they bought their last car, they go into storytelling mode. This opens up an entirely different part of the brain.[16]

They might respond, "We were expecting kids. We knew we would need a new car, but we didn't realize how overwhelming car buying can be. Not just the sales experience, but which safety features are most important? Whose safety scores are the scores that you can trust? Of course, the safest thing is probably to buy a tank, but I don't want to drive a tank, or anything closely resembling a tank. I still even struggle with the idea of owning a car."

Or another might respond, "So we really had to spend some time thinking about safety features, gas mileage, and style. It sounds awful but I was willing to sacrifice the extra loud beep if I got too close to the car in front of me if it meant I didn't look like the parents who gave up everything for their kids."

These answers reveal so much more about the consumer than we could ever understand through traditional market research. Stories have a range of moments and experiences; a continuum of a beginning, middle, and end; a character, a conflict, a tension, and a resolution. While an answer to a question is a snapshot in time, stories reveal a person in context, in time, and in relationships. And to uncover these stories, there are three narratives that are key to understanding consumer behavior: contextual, category, and brand.

---

16   Jonathan Gottschall, *The Storytelling Animal: How Stories Make Us Human* (New York: Houghton Mifflin Harcourt, 2012): 95.

IDENTIFY THE NARRATIVE CONTEXT

When we conduct market research interviews, we always begin with the narrative context. The narrative context helps us more clearly understand the context in which behavior happens. Shouting "fire" in a movie theater when there isn't one is a violation of public safety. Shouting it as you run through the hallway of a burning apartment building could save hundreds of lives. Clearly context matters. For a more consumer-friendly example, recognizing that a person believes they have a responsibility to protect the environment may help you understand why they let their lawn die off as soon as they bought the house. Once you know the context, you can locate the drivers, barriers, goals, rewards, and consequences of that context.

If you want to understand whether consumers would purchase and consume a new easy-to-make lasagna you've designed, you have to first understand the context in which that product might be used. What do family meals mean to these individuals? Is it about decadence? Is it about bonding? Is it about exploring cultures and foods? Once you understand the contextual need, you can ascertain the kinds of products that will fulfill that role. In the lasagna example, if the contextual need is about connecting with family, you may consider engineering the product to allow for parents and children to have a hand in prep.

So what happens if you fail to identify the context? Imagine what might happen if you began research under the assumption that the family simply wanted a quick meal. In that case, you may focus on making the product easier to bake, quicker to assemble, or cheaper to produce. It would also mean that you'd miss the bigger context of the emotions at play. A *family* meal isn't necessarily the easiest, quickest, and cheapest option. Without correctly identifying the context, the cake mix manufacturer in Chapter 4 may have missed that egg that changed the entire cake-making narrative.

One example I've recently started to fall in love with is a company called SnackCrate. SnackCrate is a subscription snack box service that delivers a box of snacks from a different region of the world every month to my door. As a family that loves traveling, our excitement about SnackCrate isn't even about the food anymore. Instead it's an opportunity to visit another culture.

SnackCrate transports us to another culture through a medium that we don't often seek out during travel. For example, one may make an effort to try the baba ghanoush in Lebanon or crêpes in France but may not go out of their way to experience the junk food served at the local gas station. SnackCrate is interesting because it offers foods that almost disappear into a culture, like chips, cookies, and crackers. It offers a window into the way that culture casually thinks about food. For example, a box from Pakistan gave us rose-flavored soda and one from France offered an orange soda that tastes like real oranges.

If SnackCrate were conducting psychobiographical research, one of the things they'd do is find out what experiencing another culture means to me. From this, they could learn that we travel to expand our understanding of the world, our empathy for others, and our appreciation of other cultures different from our own. Distilled down, we travel to learn about other cultures and ourselves.

By recognizing that narrative, SnackCrate might realize when it delivers these boxes, the items it includes should push my American palate and should uncover something interesting about the culture the box represents. That's why it includes exotic snack flavors (shrimp puffs, anyone?) and a musical playlist from that country to accompany the snacking experience. Our family brings out the snack box at the end of every dinner. We read the write-up about it. We each taste it and comment on how different it is to what we're used to. We joke about the flavors each of us love or loathe. SnackCrate isn't really snacking for my family. It's travel at our dinner table.

To uncover the context, we have to prompt consumers to tell us stories about the broader experience of our product or service. When looking at your own product or service, you might be tempted to first anchor to your category. For example, SnackCrate could have anchored to "snacking." But think broader than that. If you're Ford, your context may not be automobiles, but it might be transportation. If you're H&R Block, your context may not be tax services, but it might be financial management. If you're an international aid organization, you might need to start with the context of giving or generosity rather than the category of Caribbean poverty. If you're a brand-new product or service, you may need to look at the context of behaviors you might be replacing. LifeWeb 360 may compete with funeral homes and therefore needs to look at the act of mourning—not just online memorials or funeral services.

Once you feel like you've landed on the most relevant context, then you can prompt your consumers to tell you stories about that context. Once you understand the contextual need for your product or service, you can identify the behaviors and relationships consumers pursue within that context and are relevant to your product or service. Doing so moves us to categorical narratives.

IDENTIFY THE CATEGORICAL NARRATIVES

Within every context, consumers are acting to pursue their goals, avoid consequences, or simply navigate their own emotions related to that context. This is typically where your category comes in for both you and your competitors. It's at this point in an interview when we uncover what consumers turn to to meet the needs of the context.

Categorical narratives are narrower than contextual narratives. Here we begin to learn about consumers' journeys into your industry. How were they introduced to the world of subscription boxes? What did they first do to create more moments of family bonding? What do they think about the options of kitchen appliances available to them? By turning our focus to the category, we will begin to understand not only what they think about the space your product or service might be in, but what mental models they have created for it, the expectations they set for it, and the rewards or consequences they expect to face as a result.

By understanding the category within the context, we understand what the category means to these consumers. A coffee machine could mean more to a consumer than a way to produce the drink that wakes you up every morning and early afternoon. For the consumer who is looking for moments of meditation or mental escape, the coffee machine could be the starting point of a ritual that is as powerful as any meditation app.

Consider my friend Adam. Adam and I have known each other for years. Adam is an energetic, ambitious, and creative individual who appreciates nuance in most situations. Typically, when Adam and I get together, we share a cup of coffee. But coffee to Adam is much more than a caffeinated drink (like it is to me). I am as satisfied with 50 cent coffee from the gas station as I am with a cup of the finest brew in the city. I drown it with cream to cool it off and I'm on my way.

Adam is a coffee connoisseur. Adam doesn't just have a drip coffee machine at his house. Adam has beans from small-batch roasters in Chicago. He grinds what he needs before every cup he makes. He has a Stagg electric kettle that heats the water to the perfect temperature for brewing. Adam has a beautifully crafted Chemex pour over coffee maker. And when Adam pours the hot water over the grounds, it looks like choreography. There's a pattern. A waiting period. Another pattern. When I've watched Adam make coffee, he forgets I'm there. He's in the coffee moment. For Adam, all of this coffee paraphernalia is about craft. Adam doesn't just drink coffee. He consumes the entire coffee-making experience.

But if you don't understand the context of Adam's morning rituals or coffee experiences, you don't understand what role his Chemex and Stagg products play in his life.

If we were interviewing Adam about coffee devices like kettles, coffee makers, or brewers, our first task would be to understand the context of coffee in his life. That might include story prompts such as "Tell me a story about the role of coffee in your life." From those stories, we might learn about Adam's meditative moments. Or that coffee is a magic source of focus. With an understanding of the context established, we can then turn to the category of coffee devices.

Adam may tell us stories in response to prompts such as "Tell me about the first time you brewed your own coffee" or "Walk me through when you began learning about different brewing methods." What is distinct about categorical prompts compared to contextual ones is the focus. We're not just listening for stories about coffee anymore. These stories are more directed. We're exploring the category or industry our product or service is related to.

Further, you'll notice the prompts tend to be more historical. It's about their journey through the category beginning with when they first entered the category (brewing their own coffee) to learning and exploring the category (different brewing methods).

It's also very distinctly not about a specific product or service. We're not asking them to tell us about Chemex, Stagg, or Keurig. We're following Adam's stories and the elements he mentions. We are likely to hear about these products. It's inevitable we may even hear stories about our product or service. But our focus is on understanding their relationship to the category. And when we understand that set within the context, then we can move to our final set of narratives, the brand narratives.

IDENTIFY THE BRAND NARRATIVES

The last set of narratives to collect are the brand narratives. Brand narratives are the most specific of the three narratives we collect. This is where we begin to understand how consumers relate to each of the products or services to meet the needs of the context and as tools within the category. Why do they prefer the Noom app over Jenny Craig? How do they feel about Uber compared to Lyft? What role does their Hey Humans deodorant play in their lives? By collecting the stories about the brand, we can answer these questions and more.

For some, Noom may let them feel like they're approaching weight loss from the perspective of a psychologist rather than as a temporary fad. To them, Noom may be their personal food therapist rather than a diet coach or cheerleader. Lyft may help them express their patriotic passion by connecting to its programs that give voters rides to the polls. And using Hey Humans deodorant, which is produced and packaged with the environment in mind, may help them smell fresh and declare their identity as a green shopper. The power of these stories is how they uncover both what a product does (or doesn't do) and why that matters.

Years ago I worked on a project for a major manufacturer of home printers. They were trying to understand how consumers felt about their product and what they could do to improve the experience. We interviewed people who print for all sorts of reasons at home. Aligned with the three narratives I have detailed so far (though before this model was even formed), we began by understanding the role of printing in their lives—not printers.

Consumers told us about meeting deadlines, finalizing contracts for their business, and printing creative projects like scrapbook pages, amateur architectural drawings, or digital artwork. We realized printing wasn't just the act of dropping ink onto paper. Printing brought their ideas out of the ephemeral and temporary world of the digital into the real one. Some described it as the moment they gave birth to the idea they'd been developing for years and could finally hold for the first time.

When they told us stories about printing, they told us that navigating printers wasn't easy. There were lots of features that varied between models. There were different resolutions to consider. There were aisles at Best Buy that featured printers of all sorts. While consumers wanted to bring their ideas to life, learning about and buying a printer felt like studying for a major exam. There was too much material to learn and not enough time.

Finally, we learned about the printers they ultimately chose for their home. Many began with frustrating stories of trying to set it up. There was software to install (some that they would never use) and too many buttons and unnecessary features. But the stories that stood out most were about the paper tray. Consumers complained it often broke, dumping and mixing pages and pages on the floor, turning the entire process into a nightmare.

It was this final point when a light bulb turned on for the client. They admitted that when it comes to cost savings, the paper tray is typically the first area to get squeezed. They were thinner, flimsier, and less effective than previous models. While the manufacturer was focused on adding features (that they realized consumers did not want), they were essentially destroying the experience of the consumer. We all realized that the paper tray wasn't just a paper tray—it was the birthing pod of an idea that a consumer may have been working on for months. When the tray unceremoniously let the idea fall to the floor before the consumer ever touched it, it felt like an obstetrician dropping a newborn before they could hand it to the parents. With this new focus in mind, the manufacturer learned the relationship they could have with consumers and things they needed to do to strengthen that relationship.

That's the power of three narratives in gestalt. While any one of the narratives could reveal some really fascinating insights, psychobiographical research is about understanding how each one relates to the other. Understanding the context helps give meaning to the category. And understanding the category helps reveal the importance of their relationships to individual products or services. While many clients often believe the interview doesn't really begin until the consumer starts talking about their product or service, we urge them to pay more attention to everything that comes before it. Only then can a company begin to really understand its consumers.

THREE
Narratives

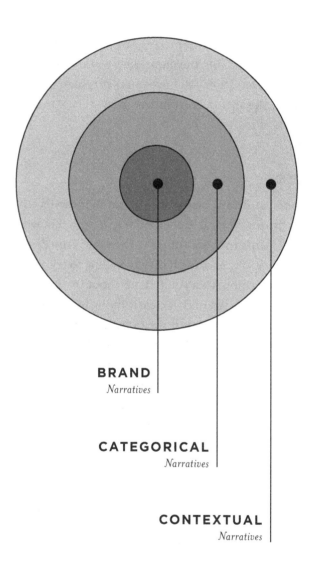

BRAND
Narratives

CATEGORICAL
Narratives

CONTEXTUAL
Narratives

ELICITING CONSUMER STORIES

Tell me a story about when you bought your first car. Tell me what inspired you to become an oncologist. Tell me a story that defines what family meals are all about.

Seems pretty simple? It is...kind of. But there are important elements to the technique that make it work so well. The better you are at asking questions, the more likely you are to uncover more in any conversation you have, market research or not. Keep these five tips in mind to improve the quality of the feedback you receive.

1. ASK LESS

It may feel odd at first to moderate a research interview that doesn't rely on questions at the center of its design. But when we ask participants to share things with us, we aren't really asking for a story. We're asking if they're willing to tell a story. Consider this question: Can you tell me about the first time you bought a car? The research is clearly trying to understand the car-buying experience, but the question can simply be answered with a yes. Maybe they'll expand on it but the question doesn't prompt the story itself. By removing the question, we can guide the discussion. Consider this statement: Tell me about the first time you bought a car. You're instantly in story mode, right?

2. AVOID QUESTIONS THAT LEAD TO ONE-WORD ANSWERS

Open it up. A lot of research tends to evaluate. Did you like the experience? Yes/No. What was your favorite feature? The auto-syncing. How did it feel? Good. These responses are all accurate but not very informative. Psychobiographical research encourages participants to expand on ideas. Tell me about the experience. Walk me through the first time you used that feature. Tell me more about what triggered that feeling for you and what it meant to you. These aren't one-word answers. These are answers that open up a conversation and provide the insight needed to fully understand the experience.

3. DON'T PRIME THEM

A major flaw in research is priming, or the concept of shaping responses through subtle or overt use of language, stimuli, or environments. Traditional research and moderators sometimes do this intentionally, but most of the time unknowingly. What did you *like* about that? What's *good* about homemade meals? Why did you pay so *much* for that? Each of these questions directs a response rather than guides a conversation. By asking someone what they liked about it, you focus them on the positives. There might not be anything good about homemade meals to the participant, but the question above forces them to find something good to say. And to the consumer, what they paid may have been just right, not so much at all. Instead, we want to limit priming in the conversation. What stood out to you about that moment? Help me understand how homemade meals make you feel. Tell me more about the value of that purchase to you. By approaching the conversation with consumers in these ways, you create an environment in which they feel invited and comfortable to tell you stories about their experience.

4. ACKNOWLEDGE THE GIFT AND VULNERABILITY OF STORYTELLING

Storytelling can be a social exercise. When people tell stories, especially about their own lives, they're constantly looking for feedback about their story. Rather than judging the stories we hear as good or bad, we should recognize them as human and understandable. This means responding with empathy. Smiling when they smile. Showing care when they voice frustration or difficulty. While we want to avoid priming participants, we can reinforce their role as storyteller by being an appreciative and receptive audience.

5. ASSUME A BEGINNER'S MINDSET

The real secret to understanding someone's perspective is actually quite simple: let them tell you about it. Too often in research, moderators will finish participants' sentences or stories. Or move on from a powerful moment in the interview without probing further. Or they'll assume they understand why someone did something, why they felt the way they did, and what they accomplished from it. Rather than playing mind reader, the moderator with the beginner's mind asks participants to explain. They probe into topics rather than making assumptions about it. When a participant tells you that the experience made them feel good, ask them why it made them feel good. Or to explain what good means to them. Always respond to the question "You know what I mean?" by revealing that you may not. That phrase is often a shortcut to avoid explaining what is really meant—but is also a door to understanding so much more.

FINDING THE PATTERNS IN THE STORIES

Once you start to gather stories, you can then begin to look for patterns. Every story typically includes the following elements, and you should keep track of what you're hearing in each of these groups.

HEROES

How does the consumer describe themselves in the story? Are they victims or victors? Partners, sleuths, or explorers? Listen for how consumers describe themselves either directly or based on their relationships with others. For example, in healthcare research most consumers will assume a deferential relationship to their physicians. But the spouse of someone diagnosed with cancer will sometimes turn into taskmaster or proxy healthcare provider. These roles will help you understand the consumer's relationship to the entire narrative and the potential relationship you might be able to build with them.

GOALS

In their story, what is the consumer trying to accomplish? Almost all stories related to consumer behavior include some sort of goal. Are they looking for a moment of respite? Are they trying to solve a problem? Are they pursuing a certain feeling? Understanding your consumer's goals will help you understand what you're really helping them do.

ACTIONS

What's happening? Understanding what's going on in a moment or an experience is one of the core objectives of most research.

What behaviors do consumers exhibit when cooking that meal? What's their experience like at the store? When you begin to recognize the patterns of behaviors across consumers in a story, you'll identify areas that are inconsistent in the experience, whether they are a struggle or seem to unfold with a great deal of ease. Further, behaviors tend to trigger emotions in the story and vice versa. So when you focus on the behaviors, you can anchor your understanding of what the emotions inspire—and uncover what could be the cause of those emotions.

EMOTIONS

What are they feeling? When analyzing stories, you're likely to hear common and non-descriptive feelings. Good. Bad. Happy. Sad. These are important to capture across all of your interviews. But a deeper reading of the transcripts may also reveal more subtle expressions of emotions (remember, understanding System 1 can feel like abstract art). The most powerful source of those subtle emotions will typically be revealed in metaphors. What metaphors do consumers use to describe an experience? Was the shopping experience an uphill battle? Did they feel like a kid again when they opened the box? Was using the app almost like meditation? Consumers use metaphors as a shortcut to explain what can be complex or hard to articulate. Digging into these metaphors will ultimately help you understand them more clearly.

Once you have all of these elements from a solid handful of consumers, your organization better understands what's happening in the space and why. In the next chapter, we'll help you take these insights and shape them into a clear story about your consumer.

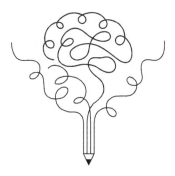

Chapter Six

The Consumer Story

In 2018, Gap released an Instagram ad for their comfort line that featured a young black mom breastfeeding her child. The story was straightforward: we sell comfortable clothes for real, everyday life. But the underlying narrative was defined, too: we want to help to destigmatize breastfeeding.

The ad didn't say that Gap has solved breastfeeding challenges or the ridiculous stigma around breastfeeding in public. Instead, they chose to celebrate one person breastfeeding on a platform where similar images are often flagged as pornography. In this way, they positioned themselves as an ally in the *customer's* story.

For those that share Gap's perspective on breastfeeding and motherhood, it's clear that Gap aligns with your values. Gap, even on top of the functional elements of the clothing being comfortable and easy to pull down for breastfeeding, is in tune with your needs.

A shaving company named Harry's ran an ad about a young boy who lost his father and was navigating what it meant to be a man. The campaign focused on discussing the idea of manhood and what it means in today's society. Harry's didn't claim to have solved toxic masculinity or to know the answer of what a man should be or look like, but rather emphasized the boy on his journey.

The narrative was subtle but clear: we support your exploration of whatever being a man could mean to you. Beyond the quality of its razors, Harry's was here to say that shaving can oftentimes be considered a symbol of manhood, but we know that manhood can't easily be defined as any single thing. However you decide to embrace manhood, if at all, we support you.

As a marketer, how do you create the kind of narratives like Gap and Harry's that allow your customers to tell their own stories? How do you give them the space to build a strong relationship with you around a greater purpose? The key is to understand that every story has a hero.

It just isn't *you*.

THE REAL HERO OF THE STORY

Because you are reading this book, it's likely that you are the CEO, marketer, or brand manager of an organization. Hopefully, you work in a business or industry you're passionate about. And that passion often becomes genuine love for your products and services. And when you really love something, all you want to do is tell the world.

But that love can be a trap.

Marketers often make the mistake of designing campaigns that tell the story of just how incredible their product is from their perspective. But the problem is that a story can only have one hero. And if you allow your product to take that important role, it doesn't allow any space for your customer to be the hero of their own story.

In 2017 Pepsi released an ad called "Live for Now," which featured Kendall Jenner. At the time the globe was experiencing a wave of social justice uprisings that protested inequality and police brutality. Pepsi's commercial opens with what can only be described as a happy kind of march with a few shots of artists (all drinking Pepsi) working in their studios nearby. The protesters hold up signs with the peace symbol, hearts, and calls to "join the conversation."

As the protesters walk down the street, smiling, nearby artists see the crowd and join. Soon everyone is dancing, playing music, and enjoying a "protest" that looks like a modern-day Woodstock. What exactly are they protesting? We aren't sure, and it doesn't seem like they are either.

About halfway in, the protesters pass by a blissfully unaware Kendall Jenner posing for a fashion shoot. She looks on in confusion at the crowd. One of the artists in the march smiles at her and nods. Without any explanation, Kendall sheds her high-fashion outfit, opting for a more approachable pair of jeans, and joins in.

Kendall smiles and weaves through the crowd, Pepsi in hand.

The protestors seem to be aware that they're standing across the street from police, who appear non-threatening without a shield, helmet, or baton in sight. The only difference between them and the crowd is the fact that they are in uniform and decidedly *not* smiling (or drinking Pepsi).

Kendall fist-bumps a smiling protester before walking up to a police officer and offering him a Pepsi. The officer accepts it, opens it, and the entire crowd cheers. No one is worried now that they are drinking soda.

One of the many problems with that campaign—even if you don't bother to unpack all of the social justice issues at play—is that Pepsi positioned itself at the center of that story. Its narrative was "we bring peace" or maybe "everyone loves us." Neither of those statements are true, and placed with a backdrop of social justice, it came off as completely out of touch with reality and a ploy by corporate America to capitalize on a major movement.

Why would a beverage manufacturer imply that the injustices that these people were protesting didn't matter anymore because of a Pepsi? Or that because everyone loves Pepsi, they somehow no longer disagree along political lines? That a famous person handing an officer a can of soda could end police brutality?

It was a weird and narcissistic ad, and customers across political divisions unanimously hated it. Pepsi wrongly positioned themselves as the hero that could end protests, rather than as a soda friends can share while watching a game. Not only did Pepsi overestimate the role it plays in people's lives, but it trivialized the very movement it wanted to capitalize on. Pepsi received so much backlash that it had to pull the ad and issue an apology.

Compare the Pepsi ad to another beverage company that positioned the customer as the hero.

In the first scene of Bell's whisky's commercial "Reader," we watch as a man catches a glimpse of a book featured in a bookstore. Next we see a montage of him attending adult literacy classes and learning to read and write. He starts leaving little notes on the fridge for his wife and playing Scrabble with his friends. Soon he is reading children's books and checking out more and more material from the library.

When he returns to the bookstore from the opening of the commercial, he buys the book that was featured in the window. We watch as he spends long nights devouring the pages. He ends up finishing the book seated at a bar. He then approaches a man we recognize—it's the author from the cover.

In the final scene, the man walks up to the author and says, "Son, I read your book."

The son's face pauses for a moment before he responds, "You *read* my book?" He then breaks out in a big smile, clearly understanding exactly what that meant for his father. The son then says, "Barman, get this man a Bell's."

The narrative is that special moments deserve celebrations and Bell's is there to help celebrate them. The whisky doesn't create the special moment, which leaves room for the customer to tell their own story about their personal celebration. In this example, the story is obviously the father's journey to learn to read and his relationship with his son. But for the audience, it allows them the space to imagine the kinds of occasions they might celebrate with a Bell's, like a college graduation or the birth of a child. Bell's narrative allows room for the customer to become the hero of their own story.

THE HERO'S PARADOX

Something surprising happens when a business stops making everything about itself and instead makes the space for its customers to become the hero. When this occurs, paradoxically, the company *does* become a hero. Let me explain.

The greatest role a product or service can play in a person's life—the most positive and productive thing it can do—is to help consumers accomplish *their* goals and overcome *their* challenges. When a business does that, it becomes a part of their lives.

When I conduct research, I'll hear consumers say things like "This is my favorite brand because it helped me through this difficult time in my life" or "I love this brand because it helped me solve a tricky problem." They begin to describe their brands as heroes in their lives because that's exactly what they are.

You Need A Budget™ is a budgeting app that syncs someone's bank accounts and other financial information to help users track income and expenses. It then helps them build a monthly budget and categorize spending.

It's designed the whole experience to center around a future of financial independence, which it defines as no longer living paycheck to paycheck, getting out of debt, and building up savings. Everything from the software it produces to the language it uses in its email campaigns is designed to help its users achieve that milestone.

I began using this app when I was young and in debt and at a time when financial independence felt incredibly far away. I was immediately hooked on its promise, but I couldn't afford the software. So it offered customers like me a free e-book that taught us how to budget in Excel. Using the book, I could soon afford to purchase the software.

Even though I've now achieved the goal I set out to, this company made such an incredible difference in my life that I remain so loyal as to continue to pay for the app to keep me on my budget and out of debt. When you let your customer be the hero, you become one, too. And once you're the hero, your customers will reward you.

Not only do I still pay for this service, but the moment anyone brings up financial independence, I bring up You Need A Budget. I tell everyone who will lend an ear about it because it truly was a hero to me.

Businesses often overlook the long-term value of the consumer relationship. They prioritize the next quarter's goal rather than playing sidekick to the consumer. So why did this company give away their information for free? Seems like a losing business model, right? They gave it away because the story was about me and my financial freedom over time. They were dedicated to *my* story, and they knew I could achieve my goals with their help. And they also understood that just because I couldn't afford their app at that time didn't mean I wouldn't be able to in the future. In that way, they set aside short-term profits to invest in our relationship.

But if the customer is the hero, then who are you supposed to be?

Branding is about becoming part of these consumers' stories and their lives. That means it's the responsibility of a brand manager or a marketing team to propose a role for their product or service within those consumers' lives. You can't just let it happen and it doesn't happen on its own. You have to figure out where you fit.

MAPPING THE CONSUMER STORY

Consider yourself as auditioning for a role in your customers' stories. Your job is to propose a role for your product or service in their lives. Based on the psychobiographical research you conduct, you can identify the opportunities in their narrative that allow you to become a part of their story.

I encourage teams to reflect on and answer these questions when crafting a brand narrative. Below we'll examine each.

1. WHO IS THE HERO?

The first question is the most basic but a critical step in any design process. Who are you designing for? Design is an exercise in empathy and the first step is to bring the person you're designing for to life.

You may be tempted to list the demographic details of your customer here. I urge you to resist that temptation. When defining the hero, begin with the kinds of details you might use to describe a friend.

- What is their name?
- What are their key personality traits and characteristics?

Years ago, I was helping a home builder better understand the individuals that purchased its homes. This was a sophisticated, nationally recognized organization that was building some of the most beautiful, high-end homes on the market. During the research phase, we immediately noticed a problem in their relationship with their clients. They called them occupants. I don't know about you, but I've never seen a doormat in front of a beautiful home that reads "Occupied." The builders had looked at their clients almost clinically. They didn't see the families that might be established, the memories that might be created, or the lives that might unfold inside these buildings. They saw numbers on a spreadsheet.

Our first order of business was to remind them that their customers didn't buy million-dollar structures just to occupy them. They bought them to make a home. From then on we focused on homeowners. Families. Retirees. Vacationers. And when we reported what we learned, the occupants became Ronny the Restless. Fran the Future-Planner. Eager Eduardo. The simple exercise of imagining the people living in the homes brought their clientele out of a blueprint and into living color.

2. WHAT IS THEIR STRUGGLE AND GOAL?

While the first question will help you define who the hero is, this next one is meant to unpack their motivations. That is,

· What struggles are they trying to address?
· What are they trying to accomplish in this context?
· What are they trying to accomplish with this category?

Remember, your product or service might not be the answer to these questions. You'd like it to be, but the focus at the contextual and categorical stage is higher-level than any specific organization or solution. This is about what the customer is trying to accomplish, agnostic of any business.

I mentioned Duolingo in an earlier chapter. If you don't remember, it's an app-based language learning software. It is different from many language learning programs in that it's not about memorizing a list of vocabulary words (think high school) or the conjugations of different verbs. Instead, it focuses on conversation because research suggests this is the quickest and most practical way to learn a language.

This app helped me master Spanish, which had been a personal goal of mine for years. And before a trip to France, I used the app to help me learn a few phrases before we landed. Now, I'm using it to learn a bit of Dutch because I've recently fallen in love with the Netherlands.

Based on the information above, what do you think is the goal of the type of consumer that might use Duolingo?

If you gave a complicated answer like "to learn a second language through a science-based process that can help users connect with another culture or avoid being embarrassed in another language," you'd be partly incorrect because you'd be defining your consumer's goal from your perspective. Not theirs.

Instead, the goal is simply "to learn a second language." Or, if we were to conduct research with language-learners, we might find that the goal is "to demonstrate to locals I appreciate their culture." At face value, this may seem like a straightforward task. But in practice, my clients get tripped up by working their products into the consumer's goal. For example, someone from New Balance might say that the goal of their customer is to wear a carefully designed shoe that will increase performance and be more comfortable. But if we're being honest, the goal of their customer is to go for a run.

Think critically about the true goal of your customers. What are they honestly trying to achieve? If they can't achieve that goal without your specific service, then it's possible you've misidentified the goal. Take your time to decide what the true goal is before moving to the next question.

3. WHAT ARE THEY DOING TO ADDRESS THEIR STRUGGLE AND ACCOMPLISH THEIR GOALS?

In psychology, goals are often thought of as motivations. And motivations are meant to inspire behavior. Working through this question, you should focus on understanding the answers to the following:

- What actions are they exhibiting?

- What products or services are they using?
- What is difficult or challenging about the behaviors?

In the customers' narrative, these answers are the meat of the story. It's one thing to be a person with a goal, but consumers consume things. People do things. To be part of the story, you have to figure out where you fit in the plot.

My Aunt Mary is in her 90s, but she's not your typical senior citizen. She's independent. She's taking courses at Temple University. She travels regularly. She's not on social media but she manages a collection of online accounts for her email, schoolwork, and healthcare. The problem is that all of them require a password.

If you were a password manager like 1Password, you'd be interested in understanding her goals when it comes to internet safety or privacy and how she manages her passwords. She doesn't want to remember the dozens of unique combinations required for each site. She finds that overwhelming and worries she might be locked out of an account forever. But she also worries someone might hack into her account.

So how does she manage her passwords? They are written down in a physical notebook on her desk. She tells me she has a formula to make them hard to guess, but anyone who's ever been hacked knows that as soon as your password has a formula, it's ripe for hacking. Aunt Mary needs a solution to her problem.

Aunt Mary in mind, an app like 1Password can begin to identify where it fits into her story. It asked her to create a master password—a single password that she won't forget that she can use for the rest of her life. 1Password takes care of the rest. So when it's time to log in to her grocery delivery service, Aunt Mary just has to remember her favorite line from her favorite poem. 1Password gives her the peace of mind that she won't get hacked or locked out, either.

By figuring out the actual events of a story—what the person is doing—you can then narrow in on how those actions make them feel.

4. HOW DO THEY FEEL ABOUT WHAT THEY'RE DOING AND WHAT THEY ACCOMPLISH?

Through the stories they've told you about their experiences, you will have a collection of emotions that describe how your customers feel through their journey. This is where you'll unpack the emotions of their story so far.

- How do they feel about the context and the category?
- How do they feel about their needs and goals?
- How do they feel about what they're doing to address their needs and accomplish their goals?

This can be the hardest part of the story to articulate because emotions can be both difficult to express and difficult to understand. If you have a collection of stories from psycho-biographical research, it may help to start with the metaphors. How do they describe the experience? How do they describe their relationship with the category? How do they describe their needs?

In a study we conducted on travelers, we asked them to tell us stories about their vacations including whether they stayed at a hotel or booked an Airbnb. They told us stories about their first time in Mexico, traveling to Japan with their girlfriend, or going back to a resort in Jamaica every year with their family. When we probed into the difference between a hotel and an Airbnb, this is what they'd tell us:

Staying at an Airbnb lets you fully immerse yourself in the culture. You're not just visiting. You're living. You're part of the community. But when you travel to a hotel, it can feel like an escape. There's something clinical, sanitary, and universal about the hotel room of a major chain hotel. It lets you escape the chaos and exhaustion of experiencing a new culture by not being part of the culture at all.

Did you notice the metaphors? For these consumers, staying in a hotel can feel almost like visiting a hospital. But notice the additional metaphors they used to describe the experience of immersing yourself in a new culture? Chaotic and exhausting. Looking at these stories, we can begin to understand that hotels may sometimes feel cold, clinical, or sanitary, but that the predictable familiarity of them can actually be a welcoming respite. Sometimes there's nothing better at the end of a long day of visiting historical sites and local markets than to make a cup of coffee and watch a rerun you love to decompress. And if you're a hotel chain, you might realize the importance of having both local items and items that feel familiar to your visitors.

With these four answers, we've now identified the core consumer narrative. Who are they? What are their needs and goals? What are they doing? And how do they feel about it?

Here's what it might look like as a complete set for one company. Let's imagine we're Lulalu, a manufacturer of intimate apparel designed for women who wear smaller cup sizes. Our goal as a consultant is to help Lulalu figure out the kind of relationship they could build with their customers. We start with their customers' narrative:

1. **Who is the hero?** Clarissa the Comfort-Seeker has been married for seventeen years. She has two kids to whom she acts as the primary caregiver. She owns and wears a variety of bras from a variety of bra makers. She prioritizes comfort.

2. **What is their struggle and goal?** Clarissa is looking for a supportive bra. She wears a 34A and her problem is that most bras gap and make her feel uncomfortable. Most of the bras available to her focus on larger cup sizes and seem to leave her to make do with bras that feel like they weren't designed with her in mind.

3. **What actions are they taking to address their struggle and accomplish their goal?** Clarissa is constantly shopping around for different bras and exploring different size combinations. She's explored bras for developing girls but doesn't want to buy bras her tween daughter may soon wear. Most of the time, she just accepts the bra won't fit well or turns to sports bras instead.

4. **How do they feel about what they're doing and what they accomplish?** Clarissa feels ridiculous shopping for bras from a site advertised to tweens. She also feels like she's been ignored by an industry that is only designing bras supermodels look good in. To her, bra shopping feels like a search for treasure that may have never been buried in the first place.

Now, Lulalu has an opportunity to find a role for their products in Clarissa's story (and the thousands of women's stories like hers). But building a meaningful relationship requires that you go further. Now, it's time to figure out where you could fit into their narrative. It's time to figure out your story.

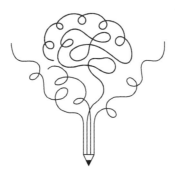

Chapter Seven

The Brand STORY

Once you've defined the relationship with the customer and understand the customer's narrative, it's time to create your brand story. This is the way you will present yourself to the world: how you'll talk about yourself, how you'll describe your customers, and how you want to be perceived. If you recall from an earlier chapter, we discussed the difference between narrative and story. Narrative is the underlying structure of your brand. The story is how you communicate or express it to the world. If narrative is the mannequin, story is the clothes it wears. While in common parlance we don't distinguish much between the two, here it helps separate two exercises that often get prematurely intertwined. Customers don't just know how you'll fit into their relationship; you have to tell them.

To help companies accomplish this goal and keep the hero at the center of their story, I've created an exercise I call the STORY framework. It helps companies organize how they talk about their organization so that it is relevant, motivating, and inspiring to customers. STORY stands for Struggle, Tools or Technology, Objective, Reward, and Yearning. The exercise is built on proven narrative structures and helps hone your brand's key idea into a single statement. With it, you'll have a valuable resource for your organization to drive messaging, creative campaigns, sales scripts, designing experiences, and more. Without it, your brand's story will be left up to your organization and customers to figure out—and they may not craft the story you intended. The rest of this chapter will walk you through each of the elements of the STORY framework and how to document it in a clear and motivating way. The first step is to identify the struggle.

S: IDENTIFY THE STRUGGLE

Great stories require struggle. A struggling character draws people in and unites them around the hero. Struggles motivate people to look for solutions. In marketing, it's the same. Every time a customer buys a product or uses a service, it's in response to some sort of problem.

"I need to relax."

"I can't find the right gift for my partner's birthday."

"I don't know how to build a treehouse for my kids."

As you craft your conflict, try to identify the core problem (not an artificial one of your making). If you're Dairy Queen, the conflict shouldn't be "people want ice cream but don't have any." If you're building board games, the conflict should be deeper than "they don't have a board game like ours." In many cases, the true conflict may have been uncovered by your research with customers and may almost directly match the conflicts we discussed earlier in the book.

A client of mine is really passionate about improving the welfare of infants born in hospitals. He admits his company is somewhat boring overall. It produces a technology to help hospitals track the health of children beyond infancy and reduce the likelihood of any medical issues down the road.

When I asked him why he does what he does, he said, "There are too many babies that are dying for no reason." This was one of the clearest articulations of a conflict I've heard from a business. It is emotional, it is clear, and it is agnostic of his business.

As we discussed in a previous chapter, conflicts should also be agnostic of your product or service. Do not be a solution in search of a problem. Find problems that exist and look for ways your business can solve them. SpotHero isn't a success because there weren't any parking apps available. They were solving a major problem as it relates to parking in the city. Finding parking can be a frustrating and expensive process that sometimes ends in failure.

When defining the Struggle for your story, try to focus on two key elements. First, make it clear. Throughout this exercise, clarity and simplicity will be key. Of course, clear is a relevant term. If you're serving astrophysicists, there are likely problems that seem painfully clear to the scientists yet sound like Latin to everyone else. Whatever the problem, be sure it is clearly and simply defined for the audience.

Second, make it emotional. Some problems aren't all that exciting. Deciding whether to put my oat milk on the shelf of the fridge isn't a struggle full of strife. However, deciding whether I should pay for an accounting platform that helps me keep my invoices paid can be a real stressor. Choosing whether to breastfeed or bottle feed can be an emotional decision for some parents. The more emotional the struggle is framed, the more powerful your solution will appear to be.

THREE AREAS OF POTENTIAL TRANSFORMATION

Figuring out which struggle consumers face can be a challenge. For many organizations, narrowing down the issues to the areas they believe they can address helps get over this first hump. The key question to ask yourself is this:

- What part of the story can your product or service transform?

This question is the key to creating a meaningful brand because the most powerful stories include a transformation. We pay attention to and engage with stories about transformation. The ordinary Frodo Baggins becomes the savior of Middle Earth. Peter Parker becomes Spider-Man. Tom Hanks is the hero in *You've Got Mail*. By focusing on what you could help transform, you become a catalyst in the consumer's narrative. Remember, you are never the hero. But you help the hero through their story.

There are three key opportunities for any brand to influence a consumer's story: their goals, actions, and emotions. And the best brands fit into all three.

Let's use the example from the previous chapter that will help us navigate this one. Here are three different ways Lulalu could help transform Clarissa's story.

Transforming Goals

Some organizations succeed by transforming the very goals consumers set for themselves. Rather than just looking for a television big enough to watch the game, an organization could inspire a consumer to seek out a way to be immersed in the full game-day experience. Rather than looking for eco-friendly detergent, a company could inspire a consumer to want clothes that require fewer washes.

What if Lulalu inspired Clarissa to want more than just a supportive bra, but a tailor-made bra she knows will fit? Lulalu's messaging, advertising, and marketing might all support Clarissa in trying on multiple bras with an easy way to return them. They may provide a customer fitting kit that helps Clarissa feel confident that she's using the same sizes and dimensions Lulalu does so when she shops, she knows she's getting a bra built for her.

Transforming Actions

No consumer experience is perfect. There may be struggles along the way. Unnecessary steps. Or adaptations consumers make to accomplish their goals. Though they still go through with the purchase, there's almost always room to improve it. By reducing barriers and making the steps to accomplish their goals easier, organizations can transform the consumer experience that leads to repeat behavior and loyalty.

For Lulalu, it may develop a bra-shopping experience that avoids that awkwardness of tween sites and the frustration of major chains. It might offer Clarissa a first set of bras of varying dimensions for her to try on. Like Warby Parker and glasses, what if Clarissa could find her perfect fit, make a note of it in her profile, and send the bras back in exchange for the styles she selected? Lulalu would have solved a number of behavioral challenges while elevating the bra-shopping experience from the comfort of Clarissa's home.

Transforming Emotions

In some cases, the goals are just right, and the actions are as efficient as they can be within corporate reason. But the experience still feels off to the consumers. It feels demeaning or flat. Or perhaps it's uncomfortable. Sometimes it feels good but not great.

A focus on the emotional experience of the consumer can oftentimes elevate the experience beyond the reach of competitors. For Lulalu, it not only makes the experience of finding a well-fitted bra easier, it also focuses on empowering women to embrace who they are. Its models match its audience in chest size. Its photos show real fits. It features actual customers and tells their stories. Shopping Lulalu feels more like joining a community of women who have struggled with the same challenges.

Combined, all three transformations can make for a powerful relationship with customers. By completing these exercises, organizations can build a road map that will direct how they build their sites, how they develop their copy, and how they design an experience that enhances the customer story.

But it doesn't just happen automatically. While these examples are clean and easy, finding the right role for your product takes experimentation. You may identify one role and find out that's not the role your customers want you to play. That's why it's important to test out different roles and different relationships with customers until you find the one that fits like a tailor-made bra.

T: DESCRIBE THE TOOLS OR TECHNOLOGY

In his seminal work, *The Hero with a Thousand Faces,* Joseph Campbell describes a hero plucked from the common world and thrust onto a supernatural journey. What many people often miss is that the hero wasn't just waiting to be called upon. Instead the hero in the best stories is reluctant to venture forth.

Further, Campbell notes that in most cultures the hero story requires some resource or act to transform the average person into the extraordinary.[17] It might be a potion from a magical sorcerer. A weapon pulled from a stone. A bite from a spider in a lab. Sometimes, it's just a bit of new knowledge that helps the hero feel like they can solve the problem.

The same holds true for your organization. Before you can aid your reluctant hero, the story needs the tool, technology, or, in some cases, approach that your organization believes makes a difference in addressing the problem.

In the Brand STORY exercise, this might be described as some new science you've identified. Perhaps you've figured out how

---

17   Joseph Campbell, *The Hero with a Thousand Faces,* 2nd ed. (Bollingen Series/Princeton: Princeton University Press, 1968): 64.

to make sustainable materials feel as soft as silk. You've identified a new technology that makes rechargeable car batteries last for a month instead of a few days.

My older brother, Dominic, runs a home health agency in South Florida. He started as a physical therapist and, with my sister-in-law Denise, grew into managing his own therapists and offering services to the elderly population in Broward County. Considering South Florida has one of the highest aging populations in the country, running a home health agency is a competitive business. The challenge in home health is that every patient needs customized clinical care. Whether it's different types of physical therapy, administration of therapeutics, or consulting on making their home more livable, each patient presents a unique puzzle to be solved.

But every patient is also an aging parent, sister, or uncle. These are people who are shifting from independence to growing dependence. And they, and their loved ones, have often returned to their home to be more comfortable, feel less like a patient, and be around their loved ones. When a therapist comes in and treats them like a patient, it's as if they brought the cold, clinical hospital system with them into the home.

Recognizing this struggle, Dominic doesn't just hire the best trained therapists and nurses. And he doesn't just run the business to be as profitable as possible regardless of actual patient outcomes (a major problem for the home health industry in South Florida). Every employee, therapist, physician, and patient that Dominic's agency works with knows about Abuelo, our late grandfather who required home health while Dominic was in training. The technique that makes Dominic's organization special is that his staff sees an "Abuelo" in every patient and treats them with the same care, consideration, and affection they might their own grandfather. The senior citizens he serves recognize it, their families appreciate it, and the physicians know that Dominic and his staff will take the best care of their patients. Dominic inspires his team to offer their patients the care he wanted our Abuelo to receive since he wasn't yet trained to offer it himself.

Whatever your tool or technology is, it should be at the heart of your competitive difference. This is what makes your product or service distinct from—and hopefully better than—anyone else in the marketplace.

O: SET YOUR OBJECTIVE

You have a tool or technology. How do you use it to address the struggle? This is your objective. The objective gives your story direction and movement. While it can be emotional, it doesn't necessarily have to be. The key thing is that it is the result of applying your technology or approach to your struggle.

Over the past decade, Domino's Pizza has experienced an incredible transformation. In 2010, its pizza was considered terrible. Customers said it tasted like cardboard. Satisfaction scores were abysmal. In blind taste tests, customers rated Domino's pizza worse if they knew it was Domino's pizza than if they didn't.[18] But unlike most chain restaurants, Domino's didn't ignore the problem or attempt to cover it with more

---

18   Adrian Campos, "Why Domino's Spent Millions to Fix Its Pizza," Insider, November 20, 2013, https://www.businessinsider.com/why-dominos-spent-millions-on-new-marketing-campaign-2013-11.

cheese. They faced it head-on and changed their own narrative to meet that of their customers.

Domino's recognized their problems but they also knew the struggle their customers were facing. How do I get a great-tasting pizza conveniently delivered? Previously, Domino's responded to this struggle by using frozen food and toppings in an effort to make the pizza as fast as possible. But J. Patrick Doyle, the new CEO of Domino's, committed himself to a better technology—producing pizza that actually tastes good. It may seem like a simple task at first, but trying to cater to the tastes of hundreds of thousands of customers can be a real challenge in the food service industry.

But ingredients and recipe weren't the only technologies Doyle employed. Domino's decided that the technology that would be at the heart of their relationship with customers was honesty. Unabashed, aggressive honesty. They agreed that their pizza was horrible. They showed focus groups and feedback. The new campaign—dubbed "We suck!"—told the world that Domino's was going to rework everything about their recipes from the flour to the sauce to the cheese to the baking process.

Using this approach to address the struggle, Domino's set the objective of winning back their customers' business and trust with the best-tasting pizza in the industry still as conveniently delivered as before. And it worked. Domino's revenue rose nearly 15 percent the first quarter of the campaign and over the years its stock has risen nearly 400 percent. Domino's shifted from having almost no story at all to one with a clear objective and one their customers understood.

This is the simple but critical task of setting an objective: to declare what your organization hopes to accomplish by applying your technology to the struggle. But the objective is rarely to just solve the problem. The most successful objectives set up the goal for the relationship and are centered on the consumer. While Doyle likely also had a personal objective to increase profit for the business, that's not what defines a relationship with customers. Earlier, my brother Dominic's objective could have been about getting more patients. But his objective, through treating every patient as if they were his own grandfather, was to provide the rehabilitation patients needed in a way that preserved their dignity and helped them feel more independent and cared for.

When you craft your objective, focus on what you hope to accomplish. While you may not be in patient care like my brother, your organization can have just as powerful an objective. If you're an app that finds qualified babysitters and completes background checks on them, your objective might be giving parents the confidence that they can trust the person they've hired. A local sushi restaurant may want their customers to feel, if just for a moment, like they're in a high-end Japanese restaurant in Tokyo. Whatever your objective may be, it will be the foundation of the reward your customers experience for engaging with your product or service.

R: DETAIL THE REWARDS

The reward is where, as the saying goes, the rubber meets the road in our story structure. With the struggle, the tool or technology, and the objective in place, we turn to detailing what the customer receives as a result.

At this point, the reward can be straightforward. In many cases, it's almost a direct response to the struggle. Domino's is going to satisfy its customers by building trust and delivering great-tasting pizzas. My brother's home health business will improve patient outcomes, recovery times, rehabilitation success, and the experience while receiving that care. But in other cases, your organization may only impact one part of the struggle. It's important to be realistic about that in the story. If you're an app that helps consumers and professionals capture and track their expenditures for tax purposes, you may not be able to increase the refund they get at tax time, but you could help make preparing for tax time a lot easier.

It's most important to identify the rewards that are critical to the story. This is not the time to list out every possible benefit identified by your sales team. Too many and the story becomes a bit boring and less believable. Focus on the one to three rewards you can provide based on your core technology, the struggle you identified, and the objective you set out for your story.

Earlier, I introduced you to my older brother and his home health agency's technology. I happen to be surrounded by successful siblings. My younger brother, Adam, is brilliant. He aced his own SATs in high school and then codified his test-taking strategies to teach them to others. The Edge in Standardized Testing helps students prepare for their tests and earn the highest score they're capable of. The students Adam and his staff serve are struggling to feel confident and prepared taking a standardized test. Adam's approach to standardized test-taking and his use of certified teachers in the field are the tools and technology that set him apart. His objective is to help students develop the skill sets and strategies necessary to become more proficient and successful at taking tests like the SATs and ACTs.

So what are the rewards in his story? Students of the Edge in Standardized Testing feel more prepared, more capable, and less anxious about their upcoming test. They get better scores and ultimately become better test-takers. Adam's organization is focused on a very narrow set of students (high school students preparing for standardized tests) and he promises to deliver a very specific reward. He's not offering tutoring for every subject and every grade level. This makes the Edge in Testing's brand story clear, concise, and relevant to his audience.

You'll also notice that the reward isn't getting a student into Harvard, Northwestern, or the University of Florida. He isn't promising parents that their children will become successful professionals in the career of their choice or responsible adults. His reward is in response to the struggle and the benefit of applying his approach to test-taking.

Articulating these rewards clearly becomes the platform for the final step in the Brand STORY process. With these rewards, a greater outcome can be accomplished—one that might transform your customers and your business.

Y: WHAT ARE WE YEARNING FOR?

The last step in the STORY framework is yearning. (I often also call this the Glorious Future but "GF" didn't fit the acronym—I'm still a marketer after all.) While I emphasized the importance of keeping your rewards realistic and grounded in the struggle, this is where we can get more ambitious and visionary. When completing the yearning for your brand story, build out a vision for a glorious future for your customers.

What is their higher calling? What would need to happen to make the struggle irrelevant or extinct? What would be the ideal outcome from using your product? By having your story yearn for something big, ambitious, and glorious, it transcends the transactional. It becomes inspiring to your customers and your organization.

I recently discovered an e-commerce site called Made Trade. Made Trade is a site that curates products that are ethically made, sustainably produced, and beautiful. They sell everything from clothing to bedding to handbags to home furnishings. I came across Made Trade after hours of looking for gifts to give my wife that fit our personal values. But trying to find and verify the ethical and sustainable standards of mainstream businesses can be a complicated and frustrating process. Made Trade recognized that struggle.

But building the site wasn't enough. Made Trade's differentiating tool or technology is their commitment to transparency about the goods they offer. They only offer products that have been responsibly sourced. Each product page tells you who the original producers are, where they are located, and their production practices. They don't just sort products by price or ratings. You can shop by value and look at products from BIPOC-owned companies or those that are handcrafted or made in the USA.

Made Trade's objective was to help consumers feel confident

that every product purchased is rigorously assessed and verified based on measures of sustainability, equity, and at least two of their eight core values. The reward of their story is that consumers can buy goods they feel good about on an easy-to-use site. They know that purse, bedsheet, or nightgown was made with vegan materials or upcycled from old products. They know their purchases will align with their values.

The story is already pretty motivating. But what Made Trade yearns for is more than a successful e-commerce site. According to their site, Made Trade believes the "world can be a more beautiful place by holding ourselves to a higher ethical standard. We call it being 'ethically elevated.' It means we put artistry above efficiency. Fair wages above profits. Sustainability above mass production. Quality craftsmanship above mindless consumption. And transparency above everything..." Now this is a story we can believe in. This is a story that a value-driven consumer wants to be part of. And it's what makes the Made Trade story so much more powerful.

When articulating what your brand story will yearn for, try to make it as dramatic as possible. This isn't just an attainable milestone. This is the ideal. The future should look and feel bigger than anything that might feel possible today in your category or industry. When it comes to defining the glorious future your story is yearning for, I always point clients toward Nancy Duarte, one of the leading thinkers in storytelling.

Duarte suggests that your story must compare the present to a beautiful future, stating that a story "needs to establish what is...the status quo. And then you need to compare that to what could be. You need to make that gap as big as possible."[19] That's how you should think about your brand story's yearning. How does it compare to the struggle defined in the first step? Is it just an incremental improvement? Or is it something that feels like a new world? Because the wider the gap between the struggle and the glorious future, the more motivating the story will be, the more your audience will want to move from one to the other.

USE THE STORY FRAMEWORK

Once you understand the theory of a Brand STORY, you can follow a straightforward framework to build your own. Use the example below and the space provided to craft your own brand story.

STRUGGLE	What is the problem, tension, or need your customers face?
TOOL OR TECHNOLOGY	What approach, technique, or resource does your organization utilize that you believe can address the struggle?
OBJECTIVE	What will you do now that you have that tool or technology to address the struggle?
REWARD	What does your customer get when you accomplish your objective?
YEARNING	What does the glorious future look like? What is the ideal outcome of using a product or service like yours?

19 Nancy Duarte, "The Secret Structure of Great Talks," TEDxEast, TED video, 18:01, https://www.ted.com/talks/nancy_duarte_the_secret_structure_of_great_talks.

Remember Lulalu from the previous chapter? The maker of intimate apparel might complete the STORY framework in the following way:

STRUGGLE	Most bra companies focus on larger cup sizes, leaving women with smaller breasts frustrated and forced to settle for a bra that gaps, looks ill-fitting, and feels uncomfortable.
TOOL OR TECHNOLOGY	One approach does not fit all breasts and bras for smaller cup sizes must be designed for real women—not just a standard definition of "petite." Design every bra from scratch and conduct repeated fit testing of each size with A-cup models.
OBJECTIVE	To provide outstanding comfort and fit, and help women look and feel their absolute best.
REWARD	A bra that's exceptionally flattering, comfortable, and well-fitting.
YEARNING	A world in which every woman feels attractive, comfortable, and confident.

In my work, I found the table above helps in tracking responses but doesn't necessarily make the story feel like a story. So, I crafted this template to bring it all together. If you complete this, you'll have a concise paragraph that describes your brand story, your relationship to your customers, and the impact you can make in their lives.

Today, [INSERT STRUGGLE]. By using [INSERT TOOL OR TECH-NOLOGY], [YOUR PRODUCT/SERVICE/ORGANIZATION'S NAME] can [INSERT OBJECTIVE]. As a result, our customers will get [INSERT REWARD] because we believe [INSERT YEARNING].

Using our Lulalu example above, we'll get:

Today, most bra companies focus on larger cup sizes, leaving women with small breasts frustrated and forced to settle for a bra that gaps, looks ill-fitting, and feels uncomfortable. By using an approach designed for real women—not just a standard definition of petite—designing every bra from scratch, and repeatedly testing each size with A-cup models, Lulalu can provide outstanding comfort and fit and help women look and feel their absolute best. As a result, our customers will get a bra that's exceptionally flattering, comfortable, and well-fitting because we believe in a world in which every woman feels attractive, comfortable, and confident.

With the Brand STORY complete, we now have the foundation for creative development, messaging, and sales. The Brand STORY clearly captures the problem, the way the organization will address it for the consumer, and the rewards and benefits the consumer can expect as a result. It defines the relationship between the product and customer and informs every interaction from the website to stores to customer service. This tool essentially becomes a filter for determining whether a marketing decision, program, or campaign supports the brand story or distracts from it.

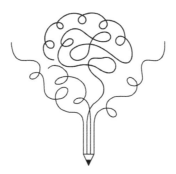

Chapter Eight

Nonprofit Narratives

While most of my examples throughout the book have been with established for-profit organizations, nonprofit organizations benefit just as much from using the STORY framework. However, there are a few nuances to the approach that have to be taken into account because of the nature of nonprofit relationships. This chapter will break down the differences and challenges of the consumer and nonprofit brand story and how your organization may overcome them.

> Note: If you're not part of a nonprofit organization, or you aren't interested in learning more about building a nonprofit brand, you can skip this chapter.

MAPPING THE DONOR STORY

In Chapter 6, we worked through the four steps of mapping

the consumer story. The donor story works the same way. Here's a reminder of the four questions we used to map the consumer story, written below:

1. Who is the hero?
2. What is their struggle and goal?
3. What actions are they taking to address their struggle and accomplish their goal?
4. How do they feel about what they're doing and what they accomplish?

The answer to the first question is very difficult for many nonprofits. What do you do when there are simply too many heroes?

TOO MANY HEROES

If your organization has a mission of serving the homeless population of your town, the hero of your organization is and should be those individuals who have been displaced from their homes. But when attempting to influence others, whether its consumers or donors, it's important to build a story where they can see themselves as the hero. That means when mapping your donor's story and building a brand story to respond to it, you should define your donor as the hero. This can feel weird at first to some organizations. And I'll talk about the risks of centering your donor in your mission. But when it comes to development and fundraising, the donor needs to be positioned as the hero of your development and fundraising stories.

Separating Your Organization's Struggle from Your Donor's Struggle

One of the peculiar aspects of a nonprofit relationship is that when a donor gives, they don't get any tangible product or service in return. They aren't trying to learn a language or struggling to do their taxes. Understanding the donor's motivations can be more complicated as a result.

From a nonprofit perspective, it is easy to assume that the donor's struggle matches the mission of the organization. If you're a food bank, you might assume that the struggle the donor is trying to address is hungry families. However, psychology tells us otherwise. While donors care about the challenges facing the world, they give because of how it makes *them* feel. Or as I heard my father Angel Alomá, a former executive director at Food for the Poor and now a consultant to nonprofit organizations, once say, "Donors don't give because your organization has needs. Donors give because they have needs."

A donor might give to an organization serving the Caribbean because they want to feel more connected to their culture. They might give to a cancer research center to honor loved ones impacted by the disease. Some may even give out of a sense of karmic energy, believing that their good fortune and luck needs to be balanced through giving to be sustained. Whatever the reason might be, it's important to center the donor story on the donor—not on your organization.

Broadening the Actions

Once you've identified the hero and the struggle, you should map the donor's actions just as we did with consumers. Donating may be your first instinct. But when you reframe the struggle to be about the donor's needs, you'll see how your answers may broaden. A donor looking to feel more connected to their culture may do so through giving, or they may engage in cultural institutions, music, and travel. Someone looking to address the literacy rates in their town may give to your organization, but they may also give to others, volunteer, or donate books to their local library. The key thing about the actions is they may not, and typically should not, be about your organization. The actions should be about how the donor addresses their struggle—not how *you* think *you* could address their struggle.

Expanding on the Emotions

As you identify the emotions that donors feel when attempting to address their struggles, it's important to note both positive and negative emotions. Donors may feel good about volunteering. But they may also feel like their impact isn't enough or they're not getting quite enough sense of accomplishment from their actions. They may feel like an ATM to their nonprofit organizations, constantly being asked to give but never feeling any sense of gratitude for their gift. In one study I conducted for a nonprofit organization years ago, we learned that giving at church felt the same as being taxed by the government. They knew it would help, but there was no positive reward associated with it. It felt more like an obligation than an act of generosity.

By identifying these critical aspects of the donor experience today, you'll begin to identify the ways in which your organization might deepen or enhance its relationship with its donors.

Here's an example of the donor story using a semi-fictional example from our work with nonprofit organizations. Take a look and see how the story is different from the consumer story and how it might relate to your own nonprofit organization:

1. **Who is the hero?** Katja is a successful CEO and grand-mother of seven. She is a native of Jamaica but emigrated to Canada for university and eventually to the U.S., where she established a life and enjoys the success of her hard work.

2. **What is their struggle and goal?** Katja recognizes the struggles facing Jamaica and the Caribbean at large. She wants to help. She also feels disconnected from her culture and wants to honor her elders who sacrificed so much for her and her life in the U.S.

3. **What actions are they taking to address their struggle and accomplish their goal?** Katja tries to visit Jamaica every other year but more and more of her family has left the island. She also gives to a charity that serves the most impoverished neighborhoods of Kingston.

4. **How do they feel about what they're doing and what they accomplish?** When Katja visits, she feels more like a tourist than a native. And though she appreciates the work the nonprofit is doing in Kingston, it feels distant to her. Katja doesn't feel much closer to the island or the Caribbean.

Notice how clearly we understand Katja, her struggles, and her motivations. From this perspective, we can already begin to see ways a nonprofit organization might relate to her more deeply or offer her more meaningful rewards for her giving. But to figure out the role we can play in Katja's story, we have to first unpack the nonprofit brand story and how Katja fits into it.

MAPPING THE NONPROFIT BRAND STORY

In Chapter 7, we used the STORY framework to identify a brand story. The nonprofit brand story uses the same structure though the perspective is slightly different. Here's the framework again with a few tweaks called out in bold for the nonprofit organization.

STRUGGLE	What is the problem, tension, or need your **constituents** face?
TOOL OR TECHNOLOGY	What approach, technique, or resource does your organization utilize that you believe can address the struggle?
OBJECTIVE	What will you do now that you have that tool or technology to address the struggle?
REWARD	What does your **constituent** get when you accomplish your objective?
YEARNING	What does the glorious future look like? What is the ideal outcome **if your organization is successful**?

Notice the small shifts. Rather than focusing on donors or consumers, you should focus on your constituents (here, they can be the hero!). This is a story about your organization after all. And the key is to make sure your organization's approach is as clear as possible. Here's what an example of the STORY framework looks like from the perspective of a nonprofit organization.

STRUGGLE	Too many children in the Caribbean are not provided the meals, education, and healthcare they need to prosper.
TOOL OR TECHNOLOGY	Our relationships with major manufacturers of food and drinks as well as with construction and building companies allow us to ship food and build simple homes, schools, and healthcare facilities in neighborhoods hit hardest by poverty in the Caribbean.
OBJECTIVE	Our goal is to build homes, provide the resources children need, and support families in creating businesses that will sustain them for the long term.
REWARD	Families that receive our services have the best chance of ending the cycles of poverty that have affected their communities for too long.
YEARNING	A world where every child in the Caribbean is born with the chance to thrive and live out their lives to their greatest potential.

As in the brand story from Chapter 7, we have a clear and concise summary of the organization, what it does, and why it matters. On its own, this is a motivating story that would likely inspire many donors to give. However, to create the best chance for success, we now have to create space for the donor in the story. And that is the key distinction between for-profit brand stories and nonprofit brand stories.

Next, the nonprofit story needs to be threatened.

THREATEN YOUR STORY

This next step for nonprofit brand stories can be the most surprising for nonprofit marketers to read about. As marketers, we're trained to always position our organization in the best light. To focus on our strengths and our benefits. But nonprofit narratives work differently. The act of giving works differently. As I mentioned earlier, donors don't just give because your organization has needs, they give because they have needs. Threatening the story creates space for the donor to meet those needs in our story.

Threatening the nonprofit story means pointing out to donors that the reward, the objective, and the yearning of the story would not be possible without their support. The struggle and the tool or technology might exist, but the organization may not be able to apply that technology without help. This is where the donor fits in. This is where the donor can feel like a hero. Threatening the story makes space for the donors to make an impact on your story.

It begins by identifying a barrier and defining a behavior.

BARRIER	What's in the way of your objective?
BEHAVIOR	What behavior can the donor perform to remove the barrier?

To identify a barrier, consider the real obstacles your organization faces. What resources do you need to perform your mission? Clarify your problems and you end up clarifying their opportunities to help.

For most organizations, the behavior they need is financial.

Generally, nonprofits know how to solve the barriers listed above, they just need the resources to be able to do so. Successful nonprofit stories use why, who, what, when, and where to prompt a very specific behavior. Below are a few examples.

	CHARITY RUN	BACK-TO-SCHOOL CAMPAIGN	SUSTAINABILITY INITIATIVE
WHY?	Increase our database	Raise funds for backpack campaign	Raise awareness
WHO?	Londoner	Parent	Individuals and businesses
WHAT?	Sign up for a newsletter	Give $100	Turn off lights for an hour
WHEN/WHERE	Right now, in Piccadilly Circus	After parent-teacher conferences	8:30 p.m. on March 26

Notice how the behavior requested is very reasonable? Someone walking around Piccadilly likely won't give up $100, but they might give out their email address. But a parent attending a specific function for their child could easily be directed to donate a generous sum in the right situation.

Below is an example of barrier and behavior for the Caribbean nonprofit in a narrative context.

STRUGGLE	Too many children in the Caribbean are not provided the meals, education, and healthcare they need to prosper.
TOOL OR TECHNOLOGY	Our relationships with major manufacturers of food and drinks as well as with construction and building companies allow us to ship food and build simple homes, schools, and healthcare facilities in neighborhoods hit hardest by poverty in the Caribbean.
OBJECTIVE	Our goal is to build homes, provide the resources children need, and support families in creating businesses that will sustain them for the long term.
BARRIER	Building homes for the thousands of children living in poverty around the Caribbean requires millions of dollars to purchase, ship, and pay a local workforce of laborers.
BEHAVIOR	We need donors to raise $1 million USD by September of this year.
REWARD	Families that receive our services have the best chance of ending the cycles of poverty that have affected their communities for too long.
YEARNING	A world where every child in the Caribbean is born with the chance to thrive and live out their lives to their greatest potential.

Again, the table is great for documenting your answers but it's helpful to convert those answers into a story you can share within your organization. Building on the template from Chapter 7, the answers above can be dropped into the following structure:

Today, [INSERT STRUGGLE]. With [INSERT TOOL OR TECH-NOLOGY], [YOUR ORGANIZATION'S NAME] can [INSERT OBJECTIVE]. But [INSERT BARRIER]. We need [INSERT BEHAVIOR]. If they do, our constituents will get [INSERT REWARD] because we believe [INSERT YEARNING].

Using our nonprofit example above, we'll get something like this:

> Today, too many children in the Caribbean are not provided the meals, education, and healthcare they need to prosper. With our relationships with major manufacturers of food and drinks as well as with construction and building companies that allow us to ship food and build simple homes, schools, and healthcare facilities in neighborhoods hit hardest by poverty in the Caribbean, Nonprofit Org can build homes, provide the resources children need, and support families in creating businesses that will sustain them for the long term. But building homes for thousands of children living in poverty around the Caribbean requires millions of dollars to purchase, ship, and pay a local workforce of laborers. We need donors to raise $1 million USD by September of this year. If they do, our constituents will get the best chance of ending the cycles of poverty that have affected their communities for too long because we believe in a world where every child in the Caribbean is born with the chance to thrive and live out their lives to their greatest potential.

Now we have both the nonprofit brand story and a role for the donor within it. This creates the most engaging relationship for donors and clearly explains to them where they fit and what they can do to feel like a hero in that story. Using this tool and the map of the donor story, nonprofit organizations can craft more motivating appeals, develop more productive stewardship strategies, and meet more of their goals as a result.

But before you run off and start applying these principles, there are some pitfalls to watch out for.

THE RISK OF DONOR AS HERO

I stated earlier that positioning the donor as the hero can feel strange but is necessary. However, it is important to put guardrails around where they are positioned as the hero so as to avoid what is more commonly referred to as "White Savior Complex."

For those that are less familiar, the White Savior Complex refers to the concept of white people—or broadly to citizens of wealthy nations—framing their generosity to charities and causes that serve minority populations as rescuing those populations. At the same time, it positions those populations as lacking agency and being in social debt to white generosity. This is especially the case in which issues and struggles these populations suffer were originally—or continue to be—caused by the behavior of those white or wealthy nations.

Consider an individual supporting the unethical trade of diamonds mined in war zones giving to charities supporting the communities affected by that industry or those wars. When we position the donor as a hero in a nonprofit story, there is a very real risk that we continue to support the savior complex.

To address this risk, there are a few guidelines I recommend when building nonprofit brand stories.

First, when defining the struggle in your brand story, it is important not to blame the populations you serve, but the systems that have created the struggle. If you're serving populations displaced from their homes, the struggle should not be about them falling into homelessness, but the lack of resources that led to them being displaced. By creating that clear distinction in the struggle—and oftentimes in your mission—you create a boundary around whom and what your donors are "saving." They are not saving the child; they are helping to restore the resources a parent needs to save their own child.

Second, when describing the donor's relationship to your organization, it is important to distinguish between their impact on your organization and the population they serve. Note that in our example above, we suggested you threaten your brand story. This creates a place for the donor to make an impact on your organization. They can be a hero in your brand story. But it is your organization, and the communities you serve, that are doing the work of your mission. Again, this distinction allows you to celebrate and be grateful for the donor's role in your organization without inappropriately placing them as hero to the communities you serve. The donor isn't saving that adorable puppy but is helping to fund the spay and neuter campaigns your organization oversees.

Third, it is important to share the stories of your constituents ethically and with dignity and respect. The stories of constituents are often presented in marketing material from a skewed perspective and often without permission. Their need. Their suffering. And then perhaps their success after the donor's gift. But that edit of the constituent story removes the work, commitment, and role of the constituent themselves. When sharing the success stories of your beneficiaries, share their complete story with their permission. Tell their story of suffering, the role of your organization and your donors, but also their act of courage, commitment, and dedication to use those resources.

I hear from many nonprofit marketers that they fear they will be unable to demonstrate their gratitude to their donors under these guidelines. That the emotional power of the story is diminished when the donor is not directly connected to the constituent. But I think this is a disservice to the donors and their ability to recognize their role in the story and to celebrate the stories of others. While donors want to feel like they're directly serving the poor, they know they are only giving a gift. But if they are able to tell stories to themselves, and to others, about the role they played in helping an organization deliver those services or resources, their story still positions them as heroes. And when they can share the complete story of the constituents served with others, they are able to borrow the power of that story and inspire others to do the same.

Above all, tread through these issues with thoughtfulness and consideration. You may not get it right the first time. But if you listen to your constituents, and to experts in the field of equity and inclusion, you will find yourself able to create stories that highlight your donors, your organization, and your constituents without sacrificing any of them.

Now that you've learned the knowledge and tools you need to create effective stories, I'd like to reflect on how we can all use that incredible power for the greater good.

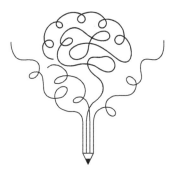

Chapter Nine

Power and Responsibility

Marketing has a massive impact on our lives. It controls the stories we hear, the ones we tell each other, and even the ones we tell ourselves. It can make us feel more confident in our bodies or more capable in our minds. It can make us feel like great parents, partners, and employees. It can make us feel proud of the things we buy and the impact our buying choices have on the world.

By framing our stories, marketing shapes the very reality we exist in.

As a marketer, part of how that world is shaped is in your hands. What will you create?

Consider this: a marketer building a story about weight loss can empower its customers to feel confident in their bodies, learn better habits, and lose weight along the way. Or it can manipulate them into believing the only way they will be loved is if they look a certain way. Both of these messages have been created by marketers and both are effective. But only one of them is a force for good.

Unfortunately, business and ethics don't always mix. From Enron to Cambridge Analytica, examples of businesses doing a disservice to the public are easy to find. At the same time, our access to personal data, a growing understanding of human behavior, and better tools of manipulation are giving businesses greater influence than ever before.

As the ones crafting these stories, we marketers stand at the threshold between businesses and their customers. We know our customers best, and we have the responsibility to represent their interests within an organization.

But we are also tasked with selling our products and services to them. Given the position we hold and the power at our disposal, it's time we held ourselves to a higher standard.

It's time we had our own oath.

MARKETERS CUT INTO PEOPLE'S LIVES IN A WAY SURGEONS NEVER COULD

You've likely heard of the Hippocratic Oath. It is a promise healthcare providers make to use their knowledge and expertise to serve the sick in the best way possible. Healthcare providers are among the most regulated professionals for good reason. Their practice can heal or harm. They have access to the most vulnerable, intimate parts of people's lives. Many people tell their physicians things they don't even tell their spouses or parents.

Because this power and privilege requires great responsibility, they take the Hippocratic Oath.

Yet, I argue that marketers have more access to more people than any physician. We know the products people buy, the shows they watch, and the websites they visit. We know how and why people make decisions. We know which features make certain apps and devices so addictive—and how to make them more addictive.

We know how to craft stories to either motivate or manipulate them into buying our products. And with the help of big data and the power of artificial intelligence, we know more than ever before. We know that people fall in love with businesses, products, and services the way they fall in love with each other. We have access into the minds of billions of people, whether they know it or not, *whether they want it or not.*

MARKETING HELD TO A HIGHER STANDARD

The world is responding. It expects more from organizations when it comes to privacy and the use of data. The EU's recent GDPR regulations are a good step and your inbox has likely been flooded with updated privacy policies as a result. Some consumers are responding on their own with campaigns to delete apps or no longer patronize certain businesses. Unfortunately, not every consumer is in a position to conduct this kind of research into the companies they support.

I began Threadline believing businesses can play a meaningful role in the lives of consumers. But we have to manage those roles with integrity, with genuine concern for society, and with a sense of responsibility to both the organizations we serve and the consumers that support them. I know many other business leaders and marketers feel the same but for there to be real change, these principles can no longer exist in the desk drawer of our consciences. They must be out in the open for all to acknowledge and expect. So, we offer this oath, adapted from the Hippocratic Oath, for you.

THE MARKETER'S OATH

I swear to fulfill, to the best of my ability and judgment, this covenant:

I will apply, for the benefit of my organization, all marketing techniques that are relevant, avoiding those twin traps of overpromising and under delivering.

I will remember that marketing is about people, as well as business, and that warmth, sympathy, and understanding those people may outweigh the organization's profit or the consumer's loyalty.

I will not be ashamed to say "Our offering won't serve you well," nor will I fail to offer alternatives when the benefits of another serve some consumers better than my own.

I will respect the privacy of my consumers, for their lives are not shared with me that the world may know. Most especially must I tread with care regarding the investment of money, time, and resources. If it is given to me to improve a life, all thanks. But it may also be within my power to ruin one; this awesome responsibility must be faced with great humility and awareness of my organization's own imperfections.

I will remember that I do not just sell a product or service but help a human being, whose needs may affect that person's family and economic stability. My responsibility includes these related problems, if I am to care adequately for the society I serve.

I will prevent wasteful spending whenever I can, for meaningful investments are preferable to thoughtless purchases.

I will respect the hard-won scientific gains of those marketers and academics in whose steps I walk, and gladly share such knowledge as is mine with those who are to follow.

I will remember that I remain a member of society, with special obligations to all my fellow human beings of different socioeconomic status, gender, race, creed, identity, and background.

If I do not violate this oath, may I enjoy a life of personal passions and professional accomplishments, respected while I live and remembered with affection thereafter. May I always act so as to preserve the finest traditions of my calling and may I long experience the joy of serving those who seek my help.

Signed,

....

I'm committed to this oath, and I hope you will too. If you take this oath, let me know. Together, we could change the world.

Acknowledgments

This book would not be possible without the love and support of so many. Thank you to all of you for being there physically or emotionally along the way.

To Courtney, Athen, and Avery, for being the best partner and children I could ask for. Without you, this would either be impossible or not worth it.

To my Abuelo, for teaching me to always bring love and generosity into everything I do. To my Abuela, Philzeets, for inspiring our family's first 'brand' and teaching me the value of hard work. To Ms. Katrin, for endowing me with the self-worth and confidence to believe I can accomplish anything.

To my mother, Deloo, for her unwavering belief in my brilliance and capabilities. To my father, Padre, for encouraging my passions and sharing his experience and expertise.

To my family, Tia, Bri, Tuna, Swigla, Superman, Brother, Niece, Scrada, Ali, Devinator, Munch, Hailey-Bug, Boo, SlickNick, Jules, and Ms. Ava, for always being there, ready to tell a story—or laugh at one.

To my best friends, Annette J., for loving me for who I am and inspiring me to be better, and Greg, for teaching me to appreciate the differences that make relationships beautiful.

To my book therapist and writer, Michelle, and my team at Scribe, including Sophie, Anna, and Rebecca, for helping me unpack my ideas and bring them to the world.

To my first hire, Madeline, for joining me when these ideas were barely ideas but believing in them anyway. To my team at Threadline, Melody and Leigh, for helping me see my ideas from perspectives I never could on my own. To Lacey, for being a sounding board that made things better and more understandable.

There are so many others who have been part of this story, my life, and my success, that I would need another book to list them. Thank you for being my bosses, my friends, my clients, my coworkers, my fellow academics, my neighbors, my colleagues, and my connections.

About the Author

KRISTIAN ALOMÁ, PHD, believes designing a successful relationship with customers requires the intentional and intelligent application of the social sciences. He graduated from Northwestern University in Evanston with a degree in Communication Science and from Fielding Graduate University with a Master's and Doctorate Degree in Media Psychology. During his two-decade career in marketing, he has helped the world's largest businesses improve their relationships with customers by drawing on his academic experience in narrative psychology, identity, and behavioral economics. At the Kellogg School Center for Nonprofit Management, Kristian is a lecturer helping nonprofit leaders learn to improve their brand narrative and enhance the donor experience through mindful design.

With Caribbean roots, Kristian is used to loud conversations, delicious food, and hot weather. Two of these things he loves—

and the other drove him to move to the cold city of Chicago. He loves talking about the world and planning trips to explore different cultures with his partner and two children.

Connect with Threadline

People make sense of the world through story. It's a core truth that defines how we at Threadline think about market research, design, and branding. By recognizing that every person is the hero of their own story, we can recognize the role our products and services play in making them feel heroic. When companies position their customers as the hero, the company becomes a part of the customer's story. So if you truly want to influence a person, you've got to first understand their story.

Threadline helps organizations identify and play a meaningful role in people's lives, through understanding the transformative power of their life stories. We do so through research techniques that uncover emotional insights, a design philosophy that focuses on the narratives people want to express, and an approach to branding that integrates your product or service into people's identities.

If you want help building a brand that does as much good for the people who use it as it does for the business, find me at Threadline.co.

CPSIA information can be obtained
at www.ICGtesting.com
Printed in the USA
JSHW080805100523
41230JS00006B/2/J